SPECTRUM

Spelling

Grade 3

Published by
Frank Schaffer Publications®

Frank Schaffer Publications®

Spectrum is an imprint of Frank Schaffer Publications.

Send all inquiries to:
Frank Schaffer Publications
8720 Orion Place
Columbus, Ohio 43240-2111

Spectrum Spelling—grade 3

ISBN 0-7696-5263-8

5 6 7 8 HPS 12 11 10 09

Table of Contents Grade 3

Table of Contents, continued

Sounds and Spellings

The short **a** sound: b**a**g, d**a**mp
The short **i** sound: p**i**g, l**i**ft
The short **o** sound: p**o**t, fl**o**ck
The short **u** sound: s**u**n, b**u**zz
The short **e** sound: b**e**d, f**e**nce

The long **a** sound: l**a**ke, st**ay**, w**ai**t
The long **i** sound: l**i**ke, m**y**, n**igh**t
The long **o** sound: h**o**me, n**o**, sl**ow**, c**oa**t, v**o**te
The long **e** sound: m**e**, f**ee**t, **ea**t, luck**y**

The /ü/ sound: r**oo**m, r**u**de, gr**ew**, m**o**ve, tr**ue**
The /ù/ sound: p**u**t, l**oo**k
The /ou/ sound: **ou**t, n**ow**
The /oi/ sound: j**oy**, b**oi**l
The /ô/ sound: s**aw**, t**a**lk, s**o**ng
The /əl/ sound: midd**le**

The /är/ sound: j**ar**, p**ar**k
The /âr/ sound: h**air**, c**are**, b**ear**
The /ôr/ sound: f**or**t, m**ore**
The /ûr/ sound: g**ir**l, h**ur**t

The /j/ sound: **j**oke, pa**ge**
The /k/ sound: **c**at, bla**ck**
The /s/ sound: **s**pi**ce**, hou**se**, **c**ent
The /z/ sound: **z**oo, u**se**, no**se**

The /kw/ sound: **qu**een
The /skw/ sound: **squ**eeze

The /th/ sound: **th**ing, wi**th**
The /wh/ sound: **wh**y, **wh**ite
The /sh/ sound: **sh**ut, **sh**ip
The /ch/ sound: **ch**ild, tea**ch**

Lesson 1 Words with the Short **a** and Short **o** Sounds

Say each word. Listen for the short **a** sound or the short **o** sound. Then, write the word.

Spelling Tips	The short **a** sound can be spelled **a**. The symbol for the short **a** sound is /a/. The short **o** sound can be spelled **o**. The symbol for the short **o** sound is /o/.

Spelling Words

bath _____

hobby _____

than _____

damp _____

bottle _____

lots _____

trash _____

flock _____

pocket _____

flap _____

Lesson 1 Words with the Short **a** and Short **o** Sounds

Words in Context

Write the missing spelling words.

Science Is Everywhere

Challenge

Circle the other words in the narrative that have the /a/ or /o/ sound.

I like science more

_____ any other subject at school. Science is also my

_____. I always keep a pen and a notebook in my

_____ to record things that I see.

Today, I went to the recycling center. I watched as old pieces of glass

that once were _____ were made into a new

_____. After that, I walked along the river. I noticed

_____ of patches of soft, green moss growing in the

_____ soil. I watched a _____ of birds looking

for worms in the ground. A few birds waded into the river and started to

_____ their wings against the water. The birds were

taking a _____, as many other animals do.

Word Building

A flock is a group of birds. Write the word from the box that describes each group of animals.

pack	swarm	colony	school
pod	gaggle	herd	bed

1. a _____ of cows

2. a _____ of whales

3. a _____ of ants

4. a _____ of geese

5. a _____ of fish

6. a _____ of bees

7. a _____ of wolves

8. a _____ of clams

Lesson 1 Words with the Short **a** and Short **o** Sounds

Fun with Words

Write the spelling word that completes each sentence and rhymes with the word in **bold**.

1. Sometimes, the ground is _____ at **camp**.

2. A _____ of crows landed on the **rock**.

3. I have a toy **rocket** in my _____.

4. You can get **cash** if you recycle your _____.

5. When I finished my **math**, I took a warm _____.

6. There are _____ of **cots** in the cabin.

7. I closed the tent _____ and lay down to take a **nap**.

Words Across the Curriculum

Say each math word. Then, write the word.

1. odd   _____

2. gallon   _____

3. fact   _____

4. pattern   _____

Write the math word that completes each sentence.

1. There are four quarts in one _____.

2. An example of an addition _____ is 7 + 3 = 10.

3. A number that is _____ can't be divided by 2.

4. The next number in the _____ 3, 6, 9 is 12.

Lesson 1 Words with the Short a and Short o Sounds

Words in Writing

Write some notes about something you have found outside. Use at least four words from the box.

| bath | than | bottle | trash | pocket | odd | fact |
| hobby | damp | lots | flock | flap | gallon | pattern |

_____

_____

_____

_____

_____

_____

_____

Misspelled Words

Read the recorded notes. Circle the four misspelled words. Then, write the words correctly on the lines below.

I found some moss growing on a tree trunk. It felt odd when I touched it. It was domp and softer then most plants. I took my hand lens from my poket and looked carefully at the small, flat plant. I could see a patten of lots of tiny green threads.

_____   _____

_____   _____

Lesson 2 Words with the Short **e**, Short **i**, and Short **u** Sounds

Say each word. Listen for the short **e**, short **i**, or short **u** sound. Then, write the word.

Spelling Tips	The short **e** sound can be spelled **e** or **ea**. The symbol for the short **e** sound is /e/. The short **i** sound can be spelled **i**. The symbol for the short **i** sound is /i/. The short **u** sound can be spelled **u**. The symbol for the short **u** sound is /u/.

Spelling Words

else _____

buzz _____

finish _____

head _____

summer _____

lift _____

ready _____

visit _____

fence _____

live _____

Lesson 2 Words with the Short e, Short i, and Short u Sounds

Words in Context

Write the missing spelling words.

Challenge

Circle the other words in the article that have the /e/, /i/, or /u/ sound.

Track Meet

Now that _____ is here, it's time for the final track meet. Students from other schools

_____ our school to run with us. Many other people who

_____ in our city come, too. They take their seats behind the

_____ next to the track. They come early, or

_____ they have to stand. You can hear the

_____ of the crowd as the runners get _____

for the race. As the race officials _____ their flags into the

air, the crowd becomes silent. Every _____ is turned toward
the runners. The flags go down, and they're off! All the people hold their

breath until the runners cross the _____ line.

Lesson 2 Words with the Short e, Short i, and Short u Sounds

Fun with Words

Unscramble the letters to make the spelling words.

1. veli _____

2. ahed _____

3. shifin _____

4. tilf _____

5. sele _____

6. deyar _____

7. muserm _____

8. efcen _____

Words Across the Curriculum

Say each math word. Then, write the word.

1. edge _____

2. hundred _____

3. nickel _____

4. minute _____

Write the math word that completes each pattern.

1. ten, _____, thousand

2. angle, _____, face

3. second, _____, hour

4. penny, _____, dime

Lesson 2 Words with the Short e, Short i, and Short u Sounds

Words in Writing

Write a newspaper article that tells about a sports event. Use at least four words from the box.

else	finish	summer	ready	fence	edge	nickel
buzz	head	lift	visit	live	hundred	minute

_____

_____

_____

_____

_____

_____

_____

_____

_____

Dictionary Practice

Each list of words begins with the same letter. Circle the second letter in each word. Then, number the words from 1–4 in alphabetical order.

1. _____ finish   2. _____ else   3. _____ hundred

   _____ flap   _____ eel   _____ hike

   _____ fence   _____ edge   _____ hold

   _____ fall   _____ end   _____ head

Lesson 3 Words with the Long a and Long o Sounds

Say each word. Listen for the long **a** or the long **o** sound. Then, write the word.

Spelling Tips	The long **a** sound can be spelled **a-consonant-e**, **ai**, or **ay**. The symbol for the long **a** sound is /ā/. The long **o** sound can be spelled **o**, **o-consonant-e**, or **oa**. The symbol for the long **o** sound is /ō/.

Spelling Words

goal   _____

fail   _____

away   _____

most   _____

alone   _____

awake   _____

chose   _____

crayon   _____

coach   _____

raise   _____

NAME _____

Lesson 3 Words with the Long **a** and Long **o** Sounds

Words in Context
Write the missing spelling words.

A New Start

Challenge
Circle the other words in the article that have the /ā/ or /ō/ sound.

After my first report card, I

decided to set a new _____. I _____ to make

sure I didn't _____ any more tests or quizzes. I knew I

couldn't do this _____. I asked my older sister to help me,

and she has been a great _____. She is helping me to

_____ my grades in _____ of my subjects. She

won't let me slip _____ to play video games. She makes me

stay _____ until I finish all my homework. She

marks the mistakes in my work with a _____.

Word Building
Verbs tell about actions. Many
past-tense verbs end in **ed**.

took	hung	laid	made
froze	spoke	came	chose

Some verbs do not end with **ed**. These are called **irregular verbs**. Look at
each irregular past-tense verb in the box. Find the present tense of the
verb in the numbered list. Then, write the past-tense verb next to the
present tense verb.

1. speak _____

2. freeze _____

3. make _____

4. lay _____

5. choose _____

6. hang _____

7. take _____

8. come _____

Spectrum Spelling
Grade 3

Lesson 3
Words with the Long **a** and Long **o** Sounds

15

Lesson 3 Words with the Long **a** and Long **o** Sounds

Fun with Words

Write the spelling word that completes each sign.

1.

2.

3.

4.

5.

6.

Words Across the Curriculum

Say each social studies word. Then, write the word.

1. vote _____   3. scale _____

2. locate _____   4. police _____

Write the social studies word that completes each sentence.

1. A map _____ can tell how many miles one inch represents.

2. The duty of _____ officers is to protect people.

3. A map helps you _____ different places.

4. Every citizen in this country has the right to _____.

Lesson 3 Words with the Long **a** and Long **o** Sounds

Words in Writing

Think about a goal that you would like to set for yourself. Write a paragraph that explains how you could meet this goal. Use at least four words from the box.

goal	away	alone	chose	coach	vote	scale
fail	most	awake	crayon	raise	locate	police

_____

_____

_____

_____

_____

Misspelled Words

Read the paragraph. Circle the five misspelled words. Then, write the words correctly on the lines below.

My bedroom is usually a mess. Sometimes, there is a trale of clothes on the floor. I can't locait anything because moste of my things are scattered everywhere. So, I'm going to set a goal to clean my room every Saturday morning as soon as I'm awaike. During the week, I'll try to put things awaye when I'm finished using them.

_____   _____   _____

_____   _____

Lesson 4 Words with the Long e and Long i Sounds

Say each word. Listen for the long **e** or long **i** sound. Then, write the word.

Spelling Tips	The long **e** sound can be spelled **e**, **ee**, **ea**, **y**, or **ay**. The symbol for the long **e** sound is /ē/. The long **i** sound can be spelled **i-consonant-e**, **y**, or **igh**. The symbol for the long **i** sound is /ī/.

Spelling Words

high   _____

easy   _____

wheel   _____

busy   _____

smile   _____

street   _____

lucky   _____

wipe   _____

might   _____

between   _____

Lesson 4 Words with the Long **e** and Long **i** Sounds

Words in Context
Write the missing spelling words.

Our Class Car Wash

<table>
<tr><td>**Challenge**</td></tr>
<tr><td>Circle the other words in the article that have the /ē/ or /ī/ sound.</td></tr>
</table>

Last week, the students in my

class had a car wash. We were afraid that it _____ rain, but

we were _____. By noon, the sun was _____
in the sky with no sign of any clouds. We set up our car wash

_____ two buildings on the main _____ in
town. A lot of people wanted their cars washed, so we were all very

_____. It wasn't _____ to scrub and

_____ off the cars until they were
clean and shiny. We even made sure that every

_____ was free of dirt. Every one of

our customers left with a _____.

Word Building
The ending –**y** is added to some nouns to make adjectives. Add **y** to each
word to make an adjective. Then, write the adjective.
Example: **luck** **lucky**

I. rain_____ _____

2. moss_____ _____

3. dust_____ _____

4. rock_____ _____

5. wind_____ _____

6. bump_____ _____

7. pick_____ _____

8. crust_____ _____

Lesson 4 Words with the Long e and Long i Sounds

Fun with Words

Write the missing vowels that complete the spelling words.

1. sm_____l _____

2. str_____ _____ t

3. _____ _____ s _____

4. w_____p _____

5. m_____ght

6. luck _____

7. h_____gh

8. bus _____

9. b_____tw_____ _____ n

10. wh_____ _____ l

Words Across the Curriculum

Say each math word. Then, write the word.

1. mile   _____

2. twice   _____

3. area   _____

4. equal   _____

Write the math words that complete the word problem.

Mike's ranch is shaped like a rectangle. It is one _____

long on two sides, so these sides are _____ to one another.

The other two sides are _____ as long as the first two. What

is the _____ of Mike's ranch?

Lesson 4 Words with the Long e and Long i Sounds

Words in Writing

Imagine your class needs to raise money for a class field trip. What ideas do you have about how to raise the money? Write the words for a poster advertising one of your ideas. Use at least four words from the box.

high	wheel	smile	lucky	might	mile	area
easy	busy	street	wipe	between	twice	equal

_____

_____

_____

_____

_____

Dictionary Practice

Look at each pair of guide words. Circle the word that comes between the two words in alphabetical order.

1. easy—elf   end   edge   equal

2. smile—spot   square   staff   spoon

3. weep—wipe   won   want   wheel

4. boss—busy   break   by   blank

5. might—must   myth   more   math

6. bath—black   between   break   both

Lesson 5 Words with the /ü/ Sound

Say each word. Listen for the /ü/ sound. Then, write the word.

Spelling Tips	The /ü/ sound can be spelled **ew**, **o-consonant-e**, **oo**, **ue**, and **u-consonant-e**.

Spelling Words

cool _____

rule _____

lose _____

noon _____

true _____

move _____

mood _____

grew _____

clue _____

scoop _____

Lesson 5 Words with the /ü/ Sound

Words in Context
Write the missing spelling words.

Movie Review

Yesterday, I went to see a

movie. It started at _____, and I was several minutes early.

I had a _____ of ice cream while I waited for Sue. There was

a new _____ at the theater that food isn't allowed inside. I

ate my ice cream outside in the _____ weather. When Sue

got there, we went inside to choose our seats.

The movie was a _____ story about

a family that was about to _____ their farm.

The crops that they _____ had died
because there hadn't been enough rain. The family was going
to have to _____ out soon. All their bills were
overdue. The _____ of the movie was mostly sad. But there
was a _____ that the ending would turn out well.

Word Building
The story is **not true**. It is **untrue**.
The prefix **un-** means *not*. When **un** is added to the beginning of a word,
the word means the opposite. Add **un** to each word. Then, write the word.

1. _____do _____

2. _____pack_____

3. _____like _____

4. _____lucky_____

5. _____safe _____

6. _____dress_____

Lesson 5 Words with the /ü/ Sound

Fun with Words

Write the spelling word that fits each meaning. Then, circle the letters to solve the riddle.

1. became bigger _____ Circle letter 1.

2. midday _____ Circle letters 2 and 3.

3. unable to find something _____ Circle letters 3 and 4.

4. a law or order _____ Circle letter 3.

5. a feeling _____ Circle letters 2 and 3.

6. to lift up and out _____ Circle letter 1.

7. real _____ Circle letter 4.

What do you call a big bird that's running free?

A ____ ____ ____ ____ ____ on the ____ ____ ____ ____ ____

Words Across the Curriculum

Say each science word. Then, write the word.

1. dew _____ 3. root _____

2. dune _____ 4. pollute _____

Write the science word next to its meaning.

1. a hill of sand _____

2. water droplets _____

3. a plant part _____

4. to spoil or make dirty _____

NAME _____

Lesson 5 Words with the /ü/ Sound

Words in Writing

Write a summary of a movie that you like. Use at least four words from the box.

cool	lose	true	mood	clue	dew	root
rule	noon	move	grew	scoop	pollute	dune

_____

_____

_____

_____

_____

_____

Misspelled Words

Read the summary. Circle the five misspelled words. Then, write the words correctly on the lines below.

    I just saw the movie *You Can't Catch Me!* It was a mystery, but it was based on a trew story. It was about a detective who kept trying to catch a spy. The mude of the movie was exciting. Every time the detective found a new clew, the suspense grue. He would be close to finding the spy, but then he would loose track of her.

_____ _____ _____

_____ _____

Review Lessons 1–5

Write the spelling word that means the same or nearly the same.

1. end _____

2. simple _____

3. many _____

4. lift _____

5. road _____

6. law _____

7. garbage _____

8. picked _____

Write the spelling word that means the opposite.

1. pass _____

2. winter _____

3. midnight _____

4. die _____

5. asleep _____

6. false _____

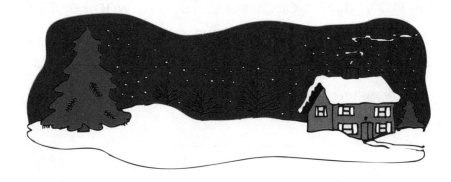

Review Lessons 1-5

Write the spelling word that belongs with each pair of words.

1. marker, chalk, _____

2. sport, activity, _____

3. face, neck, _____

4. teacher, tutor, _____

5. grin, laugh, _____

6. shovel, dig, _____

Write the spelling word that completes each sentence.

1. I fed some bread to a _____ of birds. After they ate, the

   birds flew _____.

2. We climbed over a wooden _____ to get to our

   campsite. Then, we set up our tent and closed the _____.

3. Lin gave her baby brother a _____ in the tub.

   Afterwards, she dried his _____ skin with a soft towel.

4. I'm _____ to go to my grandparents' house. I like to

   _____ them.

5. Ari scored the winning _____ in the soccer game. He

   kicked the ball _____ up into the top-left corner.

6. After I wandered along the river, I had to _____ the mud

   from my feet. Then, I walked on some soft, green _____.

Lesson 6 Words with Final Double Consonants

Say each word. Listen to the ending sound. Then, write the word.

Spelling Tips	The double consonants used most often at the ends of words include **ll**, **ff**, and **ss**.

Spelling Words

well   _____

miss   _____

puff   _____

fill   _____

smell   _____

guess   _____

spill   _____

stuff   _____

unless   _____

grill   _____

Lesson 6 Words with Final Double Consonants

Words in Context
Write the missing spelling words.

Summer Cookout

Our neighbor, Mr. Martin, always has a great cookout at the beginning of summer. It's so much fun that I would never _____ it _____ I were ill. Around two o'clock on Saturday, you can see a _____ of smoke rising from the small hill in his yard. Then, everyone knows that Mr. Martin has started to cook.

Soon, the yard begins to _____ up with people. Everyone tries to _____ what type of food Mr. Martin will serve. There's always

a wonderful _____ coming from his _____. You can't always tell what he's cooking. Still, he cooks so _____ that we all know it will be delicious. Mr. Martin doesn't mind if we

_____ our soda or make a mess. After we eat, some of us run off to do other fun _____, like play tag or kickball.

Word Building
The green ball is **small**. The blue ball is **smaller**. The red ball is the **smallest**. Add **er** and **est** to make new words that compare two or more things.

1. few   _____   _____

2. tall   _____   _____

3. light   _____   _____

Lesson 6 Words with Final Double Consonants

Fun with Words

Write the spelling words that complete the puzzle.

Down

1. to pack tightly
2. to cook on open flames
3. odor

Across

2. an answer you're not sure of
4. in a good way or state
5. to make full

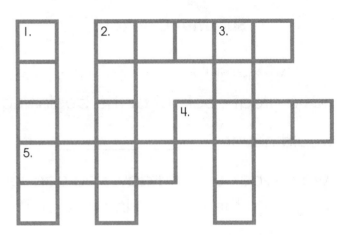

Words Across the Curriculum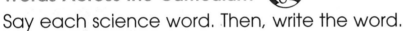

Say each science word. Then, write the word.

1. mass _____   3. cliff _____

2. chill _____   4. fall _____

Write the science word next to its meaning.

1. to make cold _____

2. the season after summer _____

3. a steep rock formation _____

4. the amount of matter in an object _____

Lesson 6 Words with Final Double Consonants

Words in Writing

Write a description of something you like to do in the summer. Use at least four words from the box.

well	puff	smell	spill	unless	mass	cliff
miss	fill	guess	stuff	grill	chill	fall

_____

_____

_____

_____

_____

Dictionary Practice

Look at the dictionary entries. Then, answer the questions.

stuff /stuf/ **n. 1.** a collection of things. **2.** the material something is made of. **v. 1.** To cram or pack tightly.

well /wel/ **n. 1.** A hole in the ground that contains a supply of water. **2.** a shaft in the ground used to pump oil and gas. **adj. 1.** To be in good health. **2.** In a good way.

1. Which word can be used as a noun and an adjective? _____

2. As a verb, what does *stuff* mean? _____

3. How many definitions for the noun form of *well* are given? _____

4. Which word has the /e/ sound? _____

Lesson 7 Words with the Final /əl/ Sound

Say each word. Listen to the ending sound. Then, write the word.

Spelling Tips	The /əl/ sound at the ends of words is often spelled **le**.

Spelling Words

settle   _____

eagle   _____

rattle   _____

saddle   _____

cattle   _____

middle   _____

ripple   _____

turtle   _____

single   _____

pebble   _____

Lesson 7 Words with the Final /əl/ Sound

Words in Context

Write the missing spelling words.

The West

> **Challenge**
>
> Circle the other words in the story that have the final /əl/ sound.

There are still places in the West where hardly any pioneers decided to _____. If you can handle a horse, you can put a _____ on him and ride out into the _____ of nowhere. You might not see a _____ person all day. You might see an _____ soaring in the sky or a herd of _____ grazing on little patches of grass. You might even hear the _____ of a snake. You might also see a rushing river tumble over huge rocks much larger than a _____. Or, you might see a _____ poke its head out of a stream and make a small _____ in the water. All of these simple things make the West a special place.

Word Building

tumble	candle	rattle	turtle

Write the word from the box that can be added to each word below to make a compound word. Then, write the compound word.

1. _____ + snake = _____

2. _____ + neck = _____

3. _____ + weed = _____

4. _____ + light = _____

Lesson 7 Words with the Final /əl/ Sound

Fun with Words

Write the spelling word that completes each sentence and contains the word in **bold**.

1. The **cat** ran away from the herd of _____.

2. The children decided to _____ down and play with a **set** of blocks.

3. I was **sad** when my horse's old _____ wore out.

4. The **rip** in the flag made it _____ in the wind.

5. That **rat** likes to _____ its cage.

Words Across the Curriculum

Say each social studies word. Then, write the word.

1. battle _____   3. castle _____

2. jungle _____   4. maple _____

Write the social studies word that completes each sentence.

1. The old _____ is protected by high, stone walls and a moat.

2. Parrots, monkeys, and snakes live in a tropical _____.

3. A _____ leaf is the symbol on the flag of Canada.

4. The two armies met in a terrible _____.

Lesson 7 Words with the Final /əl/ Sound

Words in Writing

Write a description of a place in nature that you like. Use at least four words from the box.

settle	rattle	cattle	ripple	single	battle	jungle
eagle	saddle	middle	turtle	pebble	castle	maple

_____

_____

_____

_____

_____

_____

_____

Misspelled Words

Read the description. Circle the five misspelled words. Then, write the words correctly on the lines below.

   I like to sit under the mapel tree by the pond. Sometimes, I throw a pebbele into the middel of the water. The singel ripple it makes soon turns into many other little ripples. They sometimes disturb a turtel or a frog sitting near the edge of the pond. Soon, the water is calm again.

_____   _____   _____

_____   _____

Lesson 8 Words with Double Consonants

Say each word. Listen to the middle consonant sound. Then, write the word.

Spelling Tips	The middle consonant sounds in two-syllable words are sometimes spelled with double consonants.

Spelling Words

letter   _____

dollar   _____

happen   _____

better   _____

rabbit   _____

hammer   _____

soccer   _____

dinner   _____

zipper   _____

ladder   _____

Lesson 8 Words with Double Consonants

Words in Context

Write the missing spelling words.

Shopping Trip

Last weekend, I went to the mall

to shop. I dropped a _____ in the mailbox for my mother on

my way to the mall. When I got there, I walked around looking in the shop

windows. I saw a nice jacket, but I didn't like the _____ on the

front. I like buttons _____. I also saw some funny slippers that

were each shaped like a _____ with long, floppy ears. They

were on sale for only a _____, so I bought them. I also

bought some _____ cleats.

When I got to the last shop, I saw a man on a tall _____

using a _____ to nail a sign over the door. I was afraid that an

accident would _____ if I walked under him. So, I decided

to go home. It was almost time to eat _____ anyway.

Word Building

Some nouns with one syllable and a short vowel sound double the last
consonant when **er** and **est** are added to make adjectives. Double the
last consonant in each word and add **er** and **est**.

I. wet _____ _____

2. sad _____ _____

3. hot _____ _____

Lesson 8 Words with Double Consonants

Fun with Words

Write the spelling word that fits each relationship.

1. **Steps** are to **staircase** as **rungs** are to _____.

2. **Tennis** is to **court** as _____ is to **field**.

3. **Worse** is to **bad** as _____ is to **best**.

4. **Kitty** is to **cat** as **bunny** is to _____.

5. **Lace** is to **shoe** as _____ is to **coat**.

6. **Screwdriver** is to **screw** as _____ is to **nail**.

7. **Picture** is to **paint** as _____ is to **write**.

8. **Lunch** is to **afternoon** as _____ is to **evening**.

Words Across the Curriculum

Say each science word. Then, write the word.

1. mammal_____   3. litter   _____

2. pulley   _____   4. matter   _____

Write the science word that belongs with each pair of words.

1. wedge, lever,   _____

2. mass, volume,   _____

3. reptile, bird,   _____

4. trash, garbage   _____

Lesson 8 Words with Double Consonants

Words in Writing

Write a letter to a friend. Use at least four words from the box.

letter	happen	rabbit	soccer	zipper	mammal	pulley
dollar	better	hammer	dinner	ladder	litter	matter

_____

_____

_____

_____

_____

_____

_____

Dictionary Practice

Circle the word in each pair that is correctly divided into syllables. Use the dictionary in the back if you need help.

1. dinner   di-nner   din-ner

2. accident   acc-id-ent   ac-ci-dent

3. possible   pos-si-ble   po-ssib-le

4. soccer   so-ccer   soc-cer

5. tomorrow   to-mor-row   tom-orr-ow

6. buffalo   buff-al-o   buf-fa-lo

Lesson 9 Words with the –ed and –ing Endings

Say each word. Listen to the ending sound. Then, write the word.

Spelling Tips	When a verb ends in **e**, the **e** is usually dropped before the **-ed** and **-ing** endings are added.

Spelling Words

making   _____

shining   _____

hiked   _____

having   _____

hoped   _____

skated   _____

hiding   _____

baked   _____

diving   _____

riding   _____

Lesson 9 Words with the –ed and –ing Endings

Words in Context

Write the missing spelling words.

Today was my first day at camp.

I had _____ that I

would really like it here, and I do. So

far, I've been _____ a good time. When I woke up, I looked

out the window and saw that the sun was _____. While I

was _____ my bed, two boys stopped by my cabin and

invited me to go horseback _____ with them.

First, we walked over to the main building and ate freshly

_____ muffins and eggs for breakfast.

Then, we _____ up a hill to the barn. We
rode horses around the whole camp. We saw some

campers _____ into the lake and chasing each other along

the shore. A few other campers _____ along the path by

the lake. I thought I saw some deer _____ in the woods.

> ### Challenge
> Circle the other words in the journal entry whose final **e** was dropped before **ed** or **ing** was added.

Word Building

Write the base word next to each spelling word.
Then, add the other ending to the word.

1. hiked   _____   _____

2. skated   _____   _____

3. baked   _____   _____

4. shined   _____   _____

Lesson 9 Words with the -ed and -ing Endings

Fun with Words

Write the spelling word that completes each tongue-twister.

1. My mom is _____ many more muffins.

2. Henry _____ his horse hadn't hurt her hoof.

3. Six ships sailed south under the _____ summer sun.

4. Ben _____ bread before beginning to broil the beef.

5. Skip sledded, skied, and _____ on some slippery surfaces.

6. Dan discovered a dozen _____ dolphins.

7. Hundreds of hens were _____ from hungry hunters.

8. Harry is _____ his helper hold his hat.

Words Across the Curriculum

Say each art word. Then, write the word.

1. creating _____   3. shaping _____

2. glazed _____   4. fired _____

Write the missing art words.

I like _____ things with clay. I begin by

_____ the clay into a form. Then, I put it into a kiln, where

the clay form is _____. Sometimes, I coat the form with clear

paint. This gives the form a _____ look.

Lesson 9 Words with the -ed and -ing Endings

Words in Writing

Write an invitation to a party you would like to have. Use at least four words from the box.

making	hiked	hoped	hiding	diving	creating	shaping
shining	having	skated	baked	riding	glazed	fired

_____

_____

_____

_____

_____

_____

_____

Misspelled Words

Read the invitation. Circle the five misspelled words. Then, write the words correctly on the lines below.

I am haveing a pool party next Saturday. I hope the sun is shineing so we can all go swimming and diveing in the pool. Then, I will be makeing hamburgers for dinner. We'll also have bakede potatoes. I hope you can come!

_____   _____   _____

_____   _____

Review Lessons 6–9

Write the spelling words that mean the same or almost the same.

1. hare   _____

2. creating   _____

3. odor   _____

4. stone   _____

5. supper   _____

6. note   _____

Write the spelling word that belongs with each pair of words.

1. broil, bake,   _____

2. frog, snail,   _____

3. walked, climbed,   _____

4. button, hook,   _____

5. pack, cram,   _____

6. alone, one,   _____

7. bright, gleaming,   _____

8. good, best,   _____

Review Lessons 6-9

Write the spelling word that rhymes with each pair of words.

1. mess, less, _____

2. raked, faked, _____

3. tell, sell, _____

4. locker, rocker, _____

5. rated, waited, _____

6. kiss, hiss, _____

Write the spelling word that completes each sentence.

1. A _____ of smoke rose from the fire.

2. Please use the _____ to pound the nail.

3. I _____ that I got a good grade on my test.

4. A duck was swimming in the _____ of the pond.

5. Each balloon costs one _____.

6. My dad climbed the _____ to fix the roof.

7. The _____ made a nest on a high cliff.

8. I put the _____ on my horse and went for a ride.

LESSONS 6-9 REVIEW

Lesson 10 Words with the /oi/ Sound

Say each word. Listen for the /oi/ sound. Then, write the word.

Spelling Tips	The /oi/ sound can be spelled **oi** and **oy**.

Spelling Words

point   _____

noise   _____

voice   _____

enjoy   _____

join   _____

loyal   _____

annoy   _____

choice   _____

spoil   _____

avoid   _____

Lesson 10 Words with the /oi/ Sound

Words in Context
Write the missing spelling words.

Soccer Is a Team Sport

I recently decided to _____

a boys' soccer team. I really _____ playing on the team. We

are all very _____ to one another. We _____

any kind of trouble that might _____ our joy of playing the

game. If we have a _____ to pass the ball or shoot it, we do

whatever will help the team make a goal and score a _____.

We try not to listen to people on the
sidelines who shout in an angry

_____ and make a lot of

_____. Sometimes, they really

_____ us, but we don't them
destroy our fun.

> ### Challenge
> Circle the other words in the story with the /oi/ sound.

Word Building
Add the ending **-ing** to each word below.

1. enjoy _____
2. point _____
3. join _____
4. avoid _____

5. spoil _____
6. annoy _____
7. broil _____
8. destroy _____

Lesson 10 Words with the /oi/ Sound

Fun with Words

Write the vowels to complete spelling word.

1. l_____ _____ _____l

2. v_____ _____c_____

3. n_____ _____s_____

4. _____nn_____ _____

5. _____v_____ _____d

6. p_____ _____nt

7. ch_____ _____c_____

8. _____nj_____ _____

Words Across the Curriculum

Say each science word. Then, write the word.

1. soil _____

2. oyster _____

3. boiling _____

4. poison _____

Write the science word next to its meaning.

1. an ocean animal that lives in a shell _____

2. the state of a liquid when it is very hot _____

3. a layer of earth made of small particles _____

4. a substance that is harmful to animals or plants _____

NAME _____

Lesson 10 Words with the /oi/ Sound

Words in Writing
Write a newspaper article about
a sports event you saw. Use at
least four words from the box.

| point | voice | join | annoy | spoil | soil | boiling |
| noise | enjoy | loyal | choice | avoid | oyster | poison |

_____

_____

_____

_____

Dictionary Practice
Decide which words in the box belong in each column below. Then, write
the words in each column in alphabetical order.

Words with One Syllable

_____

_____

_____

_____

_____

_____

Words with Two Syllables

_____

_____

_____

_____

_____

_____

Spectrum Spelling
Grade 3

Lesson 10
Words with the /oi/ Sound

49

Lesson 11 Words with the /ou/ Sound

Say each word. Listen for the /ou/ sound. Then, write the word.

Spelling Tips	The /ou/ sound can be spelled **ou** and **ow**.

Spelling Words

about   _____

frown   _____

tower   _____

cloud   _____

flower   _____

mouth   _____

allow   _____

shout   _____

amount   _____

shower   _____

Lesson 11 Words with the /ou/ Sound

Words in Context

Write the missing spelling words.

Money Isn't Everything

Challenge

Circle the other words in the story with the /ou/ sound.

Once, there was a king who liked to

shut himself up in the _____ of his castle. He locked the door

and didn't _____ anyone to enter. The king spent many hours

every day counting his money, but the _____ was never

enough for him. Every time he finished counting his money, the corners of

his _____ drooped down into a _____.

One day, the king heard a loud sound coming from
outside his window. He looked outside and saw a heavy

_____ of rain falling to the ground. He heard

someone _____ his name, but he couldn't see

anyone there. The king hurried down into his _____

garden. He looked around but saw no one. Even more surprising to the king,

it wasn't raining in his garden. There wasn't a single _____ in

the sky. The king sat down to think _____ this. He saw for
the first time that his garden was beautiful. He decided that he had let the
power of money rule him. From now on, he would try to enjoy other things.

Word Building

Add the word **ground** or **out** to each word below to form a compound word.

1. back _____   3. look _____

2. cook _____   4. play _____

Lesson 11 Words with the /ou/ Sound

Fun with Words

Write the spelling word that completes each sentence and rhymes with the word in **bold**.

1. You can **count** an _____ of money.

2. When the king lost his **crown**, he started to _____.

3. The thunder from the _____ was very **loud**.

4. The farmer will _____ the **cow** to go out.

5. The light spring _____ fell gently on the **flower**.

6. The children ran **out** of school with a _____.

7. The **scout** told us _____ the camp.

8. The **power** of the wind knocked down the _____.

Words Across the Curriculum

Say each math word. Then, write the word.

1. ounce   _____   3. round   _____

2. thousand _____   4. pound   _____

Write the math word that completes each sentence.

1. The smallest unit of weight in the English system is an _____.

   Sixteen of these units equal one _____.

2. When you don't need an exact answer, you can _____

   a number to the nearest, ten, hundred, or _____.

Lesson 11 Words with the /ou/ Sound

Words in Writing

Write a poem about nature. Use at least four words from the box.

about	tower	flower	allow	amount	ounce	round
frown	cloud	mouth	shout	shower	thousand	pound

_____

_____

_____

_____

_____

_____

_____

Misspelled Words

Read the poem. Circle the four misspelled words. Then, write the words correctly on the lines below.

Winter is abowt to end,

And spring is almost here.

Clowds will bring gentle shouers

To water thosands of flowers.

_____   _____

_____   _____

Lesson 12 Words with the /ô/ Sound

Say each word. Listen for the /ô/ sound. Then, write the word.

Spelling Tips	The /ô/ sound can be spelled **a**, **aw**, or **o**.

Spelling Words

because _____

talk _____

lawn _____

frost _____

dawn _____

paw _____

thaw _____

caught _____

across _____

stalk _____

Lesson 12 Words with the /ô/ Sound

Words in Context

Write the missing spelling words.

A Winter Morning

This morning, I got up at

_____. My older brother Josh was already awake. We decided to go for a walk in the woods. Josh and I put on heavy coats and

boots _____ it was very cold outside. We walked

_____ our front _____. Every

blade of grass and dried-out flower _____

was covered with _____. It wouldn't start to

_____ out until later in the day.

When we got to the woods, Josh and I stayed quiet and didn't

_____ to each other. We saw some _____

prints in the snow. We looked up and _____ sight of some deer and a much smaller, spotted fawn. The deer paused for a minute, and then they disappeared into the woods.

Word Building

Add the **-ed** ending to each word below to make the past-tense verb. Then, write the new verb.

1. frost_____ _____

2. talk_____ _____

3. thaw_____ _____

4. crawl_____ _____

5. walk_____ _____

6. haunt_____ _____

Lesson 12 Words with the /ô/ Sound

Fun with Words

Write the spelling word that answers each riddle.

1. I am cold and white. I arrive overnight. What am I? _____

2. I am green and neat. I feel good under bare feet. What am I?

   _____

3. I begin the days. I have soft, glowing rays. What am I? _____

4. I am attached to a flower. I can be straight and strong as a tower.

   What am I? _____

5. I am like a hand or foot. I sometimes make a print, but not on paper.

   What am I? _____

6. I am an action. I heat cold things. What am I? _____

Words Across the Curriculum

Say each art word. Then, write the word.

1. draw   _____   3. chalk   _____

2. straw   _____   4. gloss   _____

Write the art word that completes each analogy.

1. **Pot** is to **clay** as **basket** is to _____.

2. **Paint** is to **brush** as _____ is to **pencil**.

3. **Dull** is to **matte** as **shiny** is to _____.

4. **Drops** is to **paint** as **dust** is to _____.

Lesson 12 Words with the /ô/ Sound

Words in Writing

Write a description of a winter day.
Use at least four words from the box.

because	lawn	dawn	thaw	across	draw	chalk
talk	frost	paw	caught	stalk	straw	gloss

_____

_____

_____

_____

Dictionary Practice

Read the dictionary entries. Then, read the sentences below. Write **noun** or **verb** to tell what part of speech each word in bold is.

saw /sô/ n. **1.** A metal tool with teethlike points used for cutting. **v. 1.** To cut with a saw. **2.** The past tense of *see*.

stalk /stôk/ n. **1.** The main stem of a plant. **2.** A supporting part: the stalk of a lobster's eye. **v. 1.** To hunt or track quietly. **2.** To walk in a stiff, determined way.

1. The lion **stalked** its prey. _____

2. I **saw** the sun rise in the morning. _____

3. The teeth of the **saw** cut into the wood. _____

4. The tulip's **stalk** is tall and straight. _____

Review Lessons 10–12

Write the spelling word that means the opposite of each word.

1. smile _____

2. silence _____

3. dislike _____

4. whisper _____

5. dusk _____

6. freeze _____

Write the spelling word that belongs with each pair of words.

1. captured, trapped, _____

2. line, angle, _____

3. eyes, nose, _____

4. castle, fort, _____

5. under, over, _____

6. let, permit, _____

7. claw, hoof, _____

8. ice, snow, _____

Review Lessons 10–12

Write the spelling word that means the same or almost the same as each pair of words.

1. ruin, destroy, _____

2. total, sum, _____

3. grass, yard, _____

4. speak, say, _____

5. bother, disturb, _____

6. true, faithful, _____

Write the spelling word that completes each sentence.

1. Roses are my favorite _____.

2. Would you like to _____ our club?

3. My cat always tries to _____ dogs.

4. The _____ of a corn plant can grow to be very tall.

5. There isn't a single _____ in the sky.

6. I read a book _____ turtles.

7. The girl's _____ is so soft that it's hard to hear her.

8. I like to take a bath instead of a _____.

Lesson 13 Homophones

Say each pair of words that sound the same. Look at the different spellings. Then, write the words.

Spelling Tips	Homophones are words that sound the same but have different spellings. You have to remember which meaning fits the spelling of a homophone.

Spelling Words

so _____

sew _____

not _____

knot _____

wood _____

would _____

write _____

right _____

piece _____

peace _____

Lesson 13 Homophones

Words in Context

Write the missing spelling words.

My Tree House

Today, I finished building my tree house.

I wanted to do everything _____ and _____

to hurry, _____ the tree house took me a few weeks to

build. The floor, walls, and roof are made of _____. I nailed

each _____ together carefully. When every board was in

place, I decided to _____ my name on the door. Then, I

hung a rope with a _____ at the end down the side of the

tree. I asked my mom if she _____ make some curtains for

the windows. Now that my tree house is finished, I have a

place where I can have _____ and quiet.

> **Challenge**
>
> Circle the other words in the passage that are homophones.

Word Building

The word in bold in each sentence isn't the right homophone. Write the correct homophone from the box after each sentence.

won	wait	wear	be

1. I will **bee** back later. _____

2. Our team **one** the game! _____

3. I will **where** my blue hat today. _____

4. We will **weight** for you at the gate. _____

Lesson 13 Homophones

Fun with Words

Write the spelling words that complete each sentence. The spelling words in each sentence will be homophones of each other.

1. _____ you like to buy some _____?

2. I can _____ untie this _____.

3. Make sure that you _____ the _____ spelling words.

4. I am at _____ in this little _____ of the park.

5. Sue will _____ the rip in her dress _____ she can wear it tonight.

Words Across the Curriculum

Say each pair of words that sound the same. Look at the different spellings. Then, write the words.

1. cent   _____   5. greater   _____

2. sent   _____   6. grater   _____

3. whole   _____   7. pair   _____

4. hole   _____   8. pear   _____

Write the math homophone from each pair above that completes each sentence.

1. The number 27 is _____ than the number 24.

2. The value of a penny is one _____.

3. All the fractional parts of an object equal the _____ object.

4. A number _____ can be plotted as a point on a grid.

Lesson 13 Homophones

Words in Writing

Write a list of things you would do to set up a campsite. Use at least four words from the box.

so	not	wood	write	piece	cent	greater	pair	whole
sew	knot	would	right	peace	sent	grater	pear	hole

_____

_____

_____

_____

_____

_____

Misspelled Words

Read the list of things to do. Circle the five misspelled words. Then, write the words correctly on the lines below.

Make sure the tent is set up rite.

Chop some pieces of woud soo we can make a fire.

Wright a list of camp rules.

Enjoy the paece and quiet of nature.

_____   _____   _____

_____   _____

Lesson 14 Contractions

Look at each word. Say the word. Then, write the word.

Spelling Tips	A **contraction** is made of two words with one or more letters left out. An **apostrophe** is a mark that shows that some letters have been left out.

Spelling Words

I'd _____

he'd _____

she'll _____

you're _____

I've _____

they'll _____

weren't _____

we've _____

you'll _____

wouldn't _____

Lesson 14 Contractions

Words in Context

Write the missing spelling words.

Challenge

Circle the other contractions in the invitation.

Picnic Invitation

Dear Ben,

    I'm writing to let you know that

_____ invited to a picnic next Saturday. _____ really like you come. We're all going to meet at Riverside Park at two

o'clock. Mia and Jon are helping me plan the picnic. _____

bring the food and drinks. Mia said that _____ make

sandwiches and salad. Jon said that _____ bring soda and

ice. He's also going to bring some cookies. _____ decided to

bring my soccer ball, but my mom said she _____ let me bring my hockey sticks. She doesn't think it's a good idea.

    I think that Mia, Jon, and I have planned the picnic pretty well.

_____ invited about thirty other people. At first, we

_____ going to invite so many people. Then, we decided that we'd have more fun with a big group. I hope you can join us! I'm sure

_____ have a great time.

Your friend,
Tony

Lesson 14 Contractions

Fun with Words

Circle the two words in each question that form a contraction that is a spelling word. Switch the order of the words. Then, write the contraction on the line after the sentence.

1. Have we got time for a snack?   _____

2. Will she come to our party?   _____

3. Will you have tea with me?   _____

4. Are you ready to go?   _____

5. Have I passed the test?   _____

6. Will they come over to play?   _____

7. Would he like to see my puppy?   _____

8. Would I be able to go fishing at the lake?   _____

Words Across the Curriculum

Say each contraction. Then, write the contraction.

1. it'll   _____   3. you'd   _____

2. shouldn't _____   4. they'd   _____

Write the contraction that completes each sentence.

1. I think that _____ really enjoy reading this book.

2. The children said that _____ like to go swimming.

3. Do you think that _____ be a rainy day tomorrow?

4. You _____ go outside without a coat.

Lesson 14 Contractions

Words in Writing

Write an invitation asking a friend to
come to a picnic or party. Use at least
four words from the box.

I'd	she'll	I've	weren't	you'll	shouldn't	you'd
he'd	you're	they'll	we've	wouldn't	it'll	they'd

_____

_____

_____

_____

_____

_____

_____

_____

Dictionary Practice

Write the symbol for the vowel sound
next to each word below.

/ā/	/ī/
/ē/	/ü/

1. I've   _____

2. they'll   _____

3. he'd   _____

4. I've   _____

5. wouldn't _____

6. we've   _____

7. they'd   _____

8. shouldn't _____

Lesson 15 Easily Misspelled Words

Look at each word. Say the word. Then, write the word.

Spelling Tips	Some words aren't spelled the way they sound. You have to remember how to spell them.

Spelling Words

done   _____

other   _____

always   _____

never   _____

school   _____

learn   _____

favorite   _____

again   _____

work   _____

picture   _____

Lesson 15 Easily Misspelled Words

Words in Context
Write the missing spelling words.

I Like Art

I like to _____
about all kinds of things in

_____. Still, art is

my _____ subject. We _____ have to take a

quiz or test in art class. Instead, we just _____ on our art

projects. We don't _____ draw or paint a

_____. We also make _____ kinds of artwork.
We make shapes with clay, and weave yarn to make cloth. After we have

_____ a lot of different kinds of projects, we go back to

painting _____.

Word Building
The prefix un– means not or opposite. Add the prefix un- to each word
below to make a new word that means the opposite. Then, write the word.

1. _____done _____   5. _____fold _____

2. _____lock _____   6. _____made _____

3. _____button _____   7. _____load _____

4. _____even _____   8. _____sure _____

NAME _____

Lesson 15 Easily Misspelled Words

Fun with Words

Use the letters in each word to make at least four smaller words.

1. other _____

2. done _____

3. picture _____

4. favorite _____

5. always _____

6. learn _____

Words Across the Curriculum

Say each math word. Then, write the word.

1. square _____   3. circle _____

2. triangle _____   4. sphere _____

Write the math word that completes each sentence.

1. A _____ has three straight sides.

2. The planet Earth is shaped like a _____.

3. A _____ has four sides of equal length and four right
   angles.

4. A _____ is a single curved line.

Lesson 15 Easily Misspelled Words

Words in Writing

Write a description of a work of art that you like.
Use at least four words from the box.

done	always	school	favorite	work	square	circle
other	never	learn	again	picture	triangle	sphere

_____

_____

_____

_____

_____

_____

Misspelled Words

Read the description. Circle the five misspelled words. Then, write the words correctly on the lines below.

One of my favorete paintings is named *Rainy Night Downtown*. It's a picsure of a busy street. Squares, sircles, and other shapes represent buildings and signs. These shapes are repeated over and over agan. The colors in the painting are mostly light oranges and yellows. I've neaver seen any other painting like this one.

_____   _____   _____

_____   _____

Review Lessons 13–15

Write the contraction for each pair of words.

1. she will   _____

2. I have   _____

3. we have   _____

4. they will   _____

5. I would   _____

6. he would   _____

7. were not   _____

8. you are   _____

9. would not   _____

10. you will   _____

Write the spelling word that goes with each group of words.

1. part, segment, portion,   _____

2. correct, true, exact,   _____

3. twigs, timber, lumber,   _____

4. stitch, seam, mend,   _____

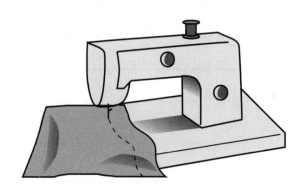

Review Lessons 13-15

Write the spelling word that means the same or almost the same.

1. trapped _____

2. finished _____

3. print _____

4. most liked _____

5. not ever _____

6. harmony _____

Write the spelling word that completes each sentence.

1. Do you ride your bike to _____ every day?

2. I like to _____ new things about the planets.

3. After the boys finished the game, they played it _____.

4. Rob missed the bus, _____ he had to walk home.

5. Can you please untie this _____?

6. There is a _____ of my dad on the wall.

7. My dog _____ like to go for a walk.

8. On the weekends, a lot of people _____ in their yards.

Lesson 16 Words with spl, spr, and str

Say each word. Listen to the beginning sound. Then, write the word.

Spelling Tips	The consonant blends **spl**, **spr**, and **str** are spelled the way they sound.

Spelling Words

splash   _____

strip   _____

strong   _____

spray   _____

stream   _____

spring   _____

split   _____

sprout   _____

spread   _____

strange   _____

Lesson 16 Words with spl, spr, and str

Words in Context
Write the missing spelling words.

Alaska

Have you ever been to Alaska in the

_____? Some of the land is still

sprinkled with snow, but a few plants are beginning

to _____. Here and there, you might

still see a _____ of frozen ground.

Alaska has many rivers. One way to see this _____ but

beautiful land is to take a boat trip on a _____. Straight

ahead of you, the water seems to _____ the land in two.

On each side, you can see the tundra _____ out for miles

and miles. You might see a salmon or other _____ fish leap

out of the water and _____ back into it a few seconds later.

These fish are so big that water drops might _____ you even
if you are far away. You can see many other splendid sights in Alaska.

Word Building
Add the ending –ing to each word. Then, write the new word.

1. sprout_____   _____

2. spread_____   _____

3. spray_____   _____

4. splash_____   _____

NAME _____

Lesson 16 Words with spl, spr, and str

Fun with Words

Use the letters in each spelling word below to make five or more smaller words with at least three letters.

1. spring _____

2. stream _____

3. spread _____

4. split _____

5. spray _____

6. strange _____

7. strip _____

8. sprout _____

Words Across the Curriculum

Say each art word. Then, write the word.

1. stripe _____

3. strum _____

2. sprinkle _____

4. straight _____

Write the art word that completes each sentence.

1. We listened to my father _____ his guitar.

2. My favorite sweater has a white _____ down the middle.

3. You can draw a _____ line with a ruler.

4. I decided to _____ some glitter on my painting.

Lesson 16 Words with spl, spr, and str

Words in Writing

Write a description of a place you have visited. Use at least four words from the box.

splash	strong	stream	split	spread	stripe	strum
strip	spray	spring	sprout	strange	sprinkle	straight

_____

_____

_____

Dictionary Practice

Read the dictionary entries and sentences. Write **noun** or **verb** to tell what part of speech the word in bold is. Then, write the number of the definition.

spring /spring/ **n. 1.** The season after winter. **2.** A spiral-shaped piece of metal that returns to its shape after being stretched. **v. 1.** To move forward or jump up quickly. **2.** To grow suddenly or quickly.

spread /spred/ **n. 1.** A cloth covering for a bed. **2.** Soft food that can be used to cover bread or other solid food. **v. 1.** To unfold or stretch out. **2.** To cover with a thin layer of something.

1. The farmer **spread** seeds over the damp soil. _____

2. A broken **spring** stuck out of the mattress. _____

3. I like cheese **spread** on my crackers. _____

4. My brother likes to **spring** out from behind a door to scare me. _____

Lesson 17 Words with the /s/ Sound

Say each word. Listen for the /s/ sound one or two times in the word. Then, write the word.

Spelling Tip	The /s/ sound can be spelled **s** or **c**. Some words have both spellings for the /s/ sound.

Spelling Words

rice _____

silence _____

sauce _____

place _____

spice _____

center _____

juice _____

erase _____

pencil _____

since _____

Lesson 17 Words with the /s/ Sound

Words in Context

My Favorite Restaurant

My favorite _____
to eat lunch is a small restaurant in the

_____ of the city. Ever

_____ my older sister first took me
there, I've really liked it. The food is simple but

very good. I usually get a bowl of _____ and vegetables

covered with a sweet _____. The cook adds exactly the

amount of _____ I like in my food.

The restaurant has a quiet patio in the back. My sister and I enjoy the

_____ of the patio and drink _____ before
we eat. Then, our server writes down our lunch order with a pad and

_____. When we change our minds, he has to

_____ the order and write it again.

Challenge

Circle the other words in the description with the /s/ sound.

SPECIALS
YUMMY SOUP
AND
SPICED RICE

Word Building

You can add the ending –**y** to some nouns to make adjectives. When a noun ends in **e**, you usually drop the **e** before adding **y**. Drop the **e** and add **y** to each noun to make an adjective.
Example: **juice**, **juicy**

1. spice _____

2. noise _____

3. ice _____

4. shine _____

5. taste _____

6. smoke _____

Lesson 17 Words with the /s/ Sound

Fun with Words

Write the letters **s** and **c** to complete the spelling words.

1. _____pi_____e

2. pen_____il

3. _____au_____e

4. ri_____e

5. pla_____e

6. era_____e

7. _____enter

8. _____ilen_____e

9. jui_____e

10. _____in_____e

Words Across the Curriculum

Say each science word. Then, write the word.

1. cell _____

2. sense _____

3. cycle _____

4. science _____

Write the science words that complete each sentence.

1. _____ is the study of the world around us.

2. A _____ is the smallest part of a living thing that performs life functions.

3. You can use your _____ of sight to observe things.

4. Water moves from oceans to clouds and back to Earth in an ongoing _____.

NAME _____

Lesson 17 Words with the /s/ Sound

Words in Writing
Write a description of a meal that you like. Use at least four words from the box.

rice	sauce	spice	juice	pencil	cell	cycle
silence	place	center	erase	since	sense	science

_____

_____

_____

_____

_____

_____

_____

Misspelled Words
Read the description. Circle the five misspelled words. Then, write the words correctly on the lines below.

One meal that I really like is chili with a lot of spise. I like to put a spoonful of chili in the senter of a bowl of risce. Then, I mix them together. I also like to have chips with my chili. I dip the chips in a cheese sause. Sometimes, I have tomato juise with my meal.

_____   _____   _____

_____   _____

Lesson 18 Words with the /j/ Sound

Say each word. Listen for the /j/ sound. Then, write the word.

Spelling Tip	The /j/ sound can be spelled **j**, **g**, or **ge**.

Spelling Words

joke   _____

gym   _____

large   _____

page   _____

stage   _____

giant   _____

range   _____

magic   _____

jacket   _____

judge   _____

Lesson 18 Words with the /j/ Sound

Words in Context.
Write the missing spelling words.

Talent Show

Challenge

Circle the other words in the description that have the /j/ sound.

Our class is planning a talent show. We

need a very _____ room to fit everyone who wants to

come. So, we decided to use the school _____ for the

show. We've just set up the _____ for the performers. We

hung a _____ curtain in front of it. We also made booklets

with the names of all the performers on the first _____.

I'm going to be the host of the show. I'll wear a black _____

and a tie. I might tell a _____ or two to make everyone feel

less nervous. My friend Gina is going to do _____

tricks. Jim will sing songs that show the _____
of his voice. We hope everyone will enjoy the show. Afterward,

the audience will _____ each performer.

Word Building

The ending **–er** often means someone or something that does something.
When you add **er** to a verb that ends in **e**, drop the final **e** before adding
er. Add **er** to each verb to make a noun.

1. joke _____   4. race _____

2. erase _____   5. write _____

3. hike _____   6. move _____

Lesson 18 Words with the /j/ Sound

Fun with Words

Use the clues to complete the puzzle.

Across

1. decide
3. a trick or riddle
5. a large, open area used to put on a play

Down

1. a light coat
2. a place to exercise
4. huge

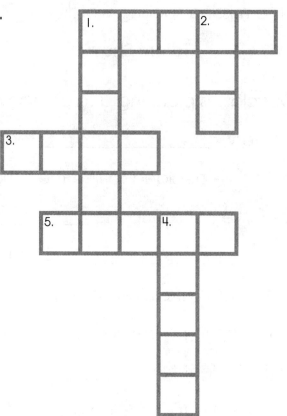

Words Across the Curriculum

Say each social studies word. Then, write the word.

1. general _____
2. journey _____
3. wage _____
4. religion _____

Write each social studies word with the pair of words it belongs with.

1. job, pay, _____
2. faith, belief, _____
3. trip, travel, _____
4. leader, army, _____

Lesson 18 Words with the /j/ Sound

Words in Writing

What kind of act would you like to perform in a talent show? Write a description of the act that you would perform. Use at least four words from the box.

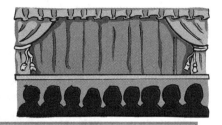

| joke | large | stage | range | jacket | general | wage |
| gym | page | giant | magic | judge | journey | religion |

_____

_____

_____

_____

_____

_____

Dictionary Practice

Write the words from the box in alphabetical order. For some words, you will have to look at the second or third letter.

1. _____   8. _____

2. _____   9. _____

3. _____   10. _____

4. _____   11. _____

5. _____   12. _____

6. _____   13. _____

7. _____   14. _____

Lesson 19 Plural Words

Say each word. Listen to the ending sound. Then, write the word.

Spelling Tip	For many nouns that end in **y**, drop the **y** and add **ies** to make the words mean more than one.

Spelling Words

penny   _____

pennies   _____

lady   _____

ladies   _____

puppy   _____

puppies   _____

city   _____

cities   _____

party   _____

parties   _____

Lesson 19 Plural Words

Words in Context

Write the missing spelling words.

My Aunt Alice

In the summer, I leave the _____ for a week and go to the

country. I visit my Aunt Alice there. She's a very nice _____

who lives by herself on a farm.

Aunt Alice loves to have _____. Last summer, her dog

had four _____. Aunt Alice invited some other

_____ to come over for a _____ to celebrate.
Two of her friends traveled to Aunt Alice's farm from other

_____. She had promised to give each one of them a

_____ to take home with them.

At the party, the children hunted for _____ that Aunt

Alice had hidden in the grass. For every _____ that we
found, Aunt Alice changed it for a quarter.

Word Building

The words in the box are
names of baby animals. Write

calf	kid	fawn	piglet
chick	duckling	kitten	puppy

the name of each baby animal next to the name of its parent.

1. dog _____
2. goat _____
3. deer _____
4. cow _____

5. duck _____
6. cat _____
7. bird _____
8. pig _____

Lesson 19 Plural Words

Fun with Words

Write the spelling word that completes each poster.

1.
Balloons For Sale
Just one _____ each.

3.
Good homes wanted for two-month old _____.

5.
Visit New York
one of the most exciting _____ in the world.

2.
Rent a peaceful cabin far away from the _____.

4.
Garden Party
3 o'clock today at the _____ Club.

6.
Have you seen this lost _____?
Reward Of $25

Words Across the Curriculum

Say each science word. Then, write the word.

1. pony _____ 3. berry _____

2. ponies _____ 4. berries _____

Write the missing science words.

1. Many children who live on farms ride _____. A _____ looks like a horse, but it is much smaller.

2. A _____ is a small fruit. There are many different kinds of _____.

Lesson 19 Plural Words

Words in Writing

Write a list of things that you would like to do on a farm. Use at least four words from the box.

penny	lady	puppy	city	party	pony	berry
pennies	ladies	puppies	cities	parties	ponies	berries

_____

_____

_____

_____

_____

_____

_____

Misspelled Words

Read the list of things to do on a farm. Circle the four misspelled words. Then, write the words correctly on the lines below.

Play with the kittens and puppes.

Take a ride on a poney.

Pick some berryes to eat.

Have a partie or go on a hayride.

_____   _____

_____   _____

Review Lessons 16-19

Write the spelling word that means the same or almost the same.

1. woman _____

2. coat _____

3. odd _____

4. middle _____

5. cent _____

6. riddle _____

7. river _____

8. decide _____

Write the spelling word that rhymes with each word.

1. flash _____

2. loose _____

3. change _____

4. guppy _____

5. long _____

6. trout _____

7. him _____

8. tray _____

LESSONS 16-19 REVIEW

Review Lessons 16–19

Write the spelling word that belongs with each pair of words.

   1. divide, separate   _____

   2. person, thing   _____

   3. theater, play   _____

   4. towns, villages   _____

   5. summer, fall   _____

   6. pen, marker   _____

Write the spelling words that complete the description.

    My family's house is in the middle of the _____, but we

have a very _____ backyard. On one side, there is a long

_____ of soil that we made into a flowerbed. In the spring,

many flowers _____ there. Sometimes, we have

_____ in our yard for our friends. We also let our dog and

her _____ run around in the yard.

Lesson 20 Days of the Week and Time Words

Say each word. Listen for vowel and consonant sounds that you know. Then, write the word. Make sure that you use a capital letter to begin each day of the week.

Spelling Tip	Many words that name the days of the week and words that tell about time are spelled the way they sound. Others have unusual spellings. You have to remember how to spell these.

Spelling Words

Friday   _____

Sunday   _____

morning   _____

Tuesday   _____

Saturday   _____

evening   _____

Monday   _____

afternoon   _____

Thursday   _____

Wednesday   _____

Lesson 20 Days of the Week and Time Words

Words in Context

Write the missing spelling words.

A Busy Week

Now that the weekend is over, I have a very busy week ahead of me. On

_____, I have to go back to

school in the _____. Then, I

have soccer practice after school. On the

next day, which is _____, I

have a piano lesson after school. There's

Challenge

Circle the other time words in the schedule.

another soccer practice the following day, on _____.

On _____, I have to go home right after school to study

for my math test. After school on _____, I'm going to visit my
grandmother. I'll have dinner with her and go home later in the

_____.

The next day is _____, the first day of the weekend.
When I get up, I have to do some chores. After lunch, I can do whatever

I want for the rest of the _____. At 7:00 that evening, our team
has a soccer match. Two of my teammates are going to stay overnight at

my house. Then, on _____, all the people in my family are
coming to my house for dinner. I have to help my mother get ready.

Lesson 20 Days of the Week and Time Words

Fun with Words

Write the spelling word that fits each clue. The words in bold will help you.

1. You might have **fried** fish on this day. _____

2. You might count your **money** on this day to make sure you have enough to last all week. _____

3. If the **sun** is shining, this might be a good day to be outside. _____

4. This is day number **two** in the school week. _____

5. There is much **more** time in a day after this time. _____

6. If you **sat** around during the week, you might have a lot of work to do on this day. _____

7. **Even** though you want to play video games, you might have to do homework during this time. _____

Words Across the Curriculum

Say each social studies word. Then, write the word.

1. early _____   3. later _____

2. history _____   4. future _____

Write each social studies word next to its meaning.

1. afterward _____

2. record of events _____

3. period of time that hasn't happened yet _____

4. near the beginning _____

Lesson 20 Days of the Week and Time Words

Words in Writing

What plans do you have for the coming week?
Write a schedule that tells what you will do next
week. Use at least four words from the box.

Friday	morning	Saturday	Monday	Thursday	later	future
Sunday	Tuesday	evening	afternoon	Wednesday	early	history

_____

_____

_____

_____

_____

Misspelled Words

Read the schedule. Circle the five misspelled words. Then, write the words
correctly on the lines below.

Sonday: Make sure that everything is ready for the school week.

Monday: Go to baseball practice in the afternone.

Tousday: Work on my art project.

Wensday: Give my dog a bath.

Thurday: Study for the science quiz.

Friday: Clean my room after school.

_____   _____   _____

_____   _____

Lesson 21 Names of the Months

Say each word. Listen for vowel and consonant sounds that you know. Then, write the word. Make sure that you use a capital letter to begin each month.

Spelling Tip	The names of months always begin with a capital letter.

Spelling Words

March _____

July _____

May _____

September _____

January _____

April _____

June _____

November _____

August _____

February _____

October _____

December _____

Lesson 21 Names of the Months

Words in Writing

Seasons

In many parts of the country, winter begins in
the month of _____, which is the
last month of the year. Often, it is cold and snowy during this month and
the two following months, _____ and _____.
Spring begins in the month of _____. Plants begin to sprout
then. They keep growing in _____, which is often a rainy
month. By _____, many plants are flowering.

Summer begins in the month of _____. The temperatures
are warm, and they become even warmer in _____. By
_____, the days are very hot. They begin to cool down in
_____, the first month of fall. In _____,
the days become chilly, and the leaves of the trees have changed to red,
yellow, and orange. By _____, most of the leaves have
fallen from the trees. Soon, it will be winter again.

Word Building

The abbreviations for six of the months are the first three letters followed by
a period. Write the abbreviations for the months below.

1. January _____   4. August _____

2. October _____   5. February _____

3. December _____   6. November _____

Lesson 21 Names of the Months

Fun with Words

Write the spelling word that completes each sentence and rhymes with the word in bold.

1. _____ is the **arch** from winter to spring.

2. _____ **will** be filled with showers so each **day** in

   _____ has many flowers.

3. We enjoy the last **ember** of every fire in the chilly months of

   _____ and _____.

4. _____ and _____ are very, **very** cold.

5. _____ goes by too **soon**, but _____ truly

   flies by.

6. Do you **remember** the colored leaves in _____?

Words Across the Curriculum

Say each science word. Then the word.

1. season _____   3. winter _____

2. calendar _____   4. autumn _____

Write the missing science words.

We use a _____ to keep track of the days, weeks, and

months of the year. Every _____ of the year has three

months. The last month of the year and the first two months of the next

year are the _____. The ninth, tenth, and eleventh months

are _____.

Lesson 21 Names of the Months

Words in Writing

Write a description of your favorite season.
Use at least four words from the box.

March	May	January	June	August	October	season	winter
July	September	April	November	February	December	calendar	autumn

_____

_____

_____

_____

_____

_____

Misspelled Words

Read the description. Circle the five misspelled words. Then, write the words correctly on the lines below.

    My favorite season is autumm. After the hot days of August, I enjoy the cooler days in Septembar. I love the shades of yellow, orange, and red on the trees in Ocober. By the end of November, I'm a little sad that wintur is almost here. But I also look forward to the holiday seson in December.

_____ _____ _____

_____ _____

Lesson 22 Names of Holidays

Say each holiday. Listen for vowel and consonant sounds that you know. Then, write the holiday. Make sure that you use a capital letter to begin each word of a holiday. Also make sure that you use an **'s** when it is needed.

Spelling Tip	The names of months always begin with a capital letter.

Spelling Words

Mother's Day _____

Thanksgiving _____

Columbus Day _____

Independence Day _____

Father's Day _____

Memorial Day _____

Labor Day _____

Valentine's Day _____

Halloween _____

New Year's Day _____

Lesson 22 Names of Holidays

Words in Context

Write the missing spelling words.

Holidays

Holidays are days of celebration that come at different times during

the year. _____ is the first holiday

of the year. It's celebrated on the first day of January.

_____

comes in the middle of February. This holiday
stands for love.

Two holidays are celebrated in May. One

is _____,

which is a special day for mothers. The other is

_____, the holiday

that honors Americans who died in wars. The special day in June for

fathers is _____.

_____ is another summer holiday. We

celebrate America's freedom on this day. _____

comes at the end of the summer. This day honors working people.

_____ is a day in October on

which we honor the explorer who discovered America. Another holiday in

October is _____. On this day, people

dress up in costumes and go from door to door saying "Trick or treat!" On

_____, we give thanks for everything we have.

Lesson 22 Names of Holidays

Fun with Words

Write the holidays next to the symbols that represent them.

1.

_____

3.

_____

5.

_____

2.

_____

4.

_____

6.

_____

Words Across the Curriculum

Say the name of each holiday. Then, write the name of the holiday.

1. Christmas _____   3. Hanukkah _____

2. Martin Luther _____   4. Ramadan _____

King Day _____

Write the holiday that completes each sentence.

1. _____ is a religious holiday celebrated by Jewish people.

2. _____ is an Islamic holiday that lasts for a whole month.

3. We honor a great civil rights leader on _____.

4. Christians celebrate _____ in December.

Lesson 22 Names of Holidays

Words in Writing

Which holidays are your favorites? Write a
paragraph that tells what you do on some holidays.
Use at least four names of holidays from the box.

Mother's Day	Independence Day	Labor Day	New Year's Day	Martin Luther King Day
		Valentine's Day		
Thanksgiving	Father's Day		Christmas	Ramadan
Columbus Day	Halloween	Memorial Day	Hanukkah	

_____

_____

_____

_____

Misspelled Words

Read the paragraph. Circle the four misspelled holidays. Then, write the
holidays correctly on the lines below.

One of my favorite holidays is Haloween. I like to carve faces in
pumpkins and dress up in a scary costume. My other favorite is
Independense Day. My family goes to a big picnic, and then we watch
fireworks. I also like Thanksgiving and Chrismas, because everyone in my
family gets together on those days. Mother Day is another special day.
I give my mom flowers and do all her chores for her.

_____   _____

_____   _____

Review Lessons 20-22

Write the days of the week in the correct order.

1. _____

2. _____

3. _____

4. _____

5. _____

6. _____

7. _____

Write the name of the holiday next to its date or description.

1. February 14 _____

2. Fourth of July _____

3. the third Thursday in November _____

4. the day in June honoring dads _____

5. the day honoring Americans who
   have died in wars _____

6. the first day in January _____

7. the day that honors people who work _____

8. the day that honors moms _____

9. the day to celebrate love _____

10. the day that honors the explorer
    who discovered America _____

Review Lessons 20-22

Write the names of the months of the year in the correct order.

1. _____   7. _____

2. _____   8. _____

3. _____   9. _____

4. _____   10. _____

5. _____   11. _____

6. _____   12. _____

Write four sentences that tell about what you like to do on your birthday. Use three spelling words that name three parts of the day.

_____

_____

_____

_____

_____

_____

_____

_____

_____

_____

Lesson 23 Words with ld and ft

Say each word. Listen for the **ld** or **ft** sound. Then, write the word.

Spelling Tip	The consonant blends **ft** and **ld** are spelled the way they sound.

Spelling Words

gift   _____

sold   _____

left   _____

raft   _____

held   _____

swift   _____

wild   _____

after   _____

drift   _____

world   _____

Lesson 23 Words with **ld** and **ft**

Words in Context

Write the missing spelling words.

Movie Review

I recently got the movie *Huckleberry Finn* as a _____ for my

birthday. The movie is about a _____ and adventurous boy

called Huck. He wants to escape from his small town and the mild-mannered

but strict Widow Douglas. He longs to see more of the _____.

Huck has an older friend named Jim, who is a slave. Jim also wants to

escape so that he won't be _____ to a new owner. Huck

and Jim escape from their town together when they _____

down the _____ water of the Mississippi River on a

_____ made of logs _____ together by ropes.

_____ they _____ their small town, Huck and

Jim had many adventures on the river.

Word Building

The suffix –**ness** means the **state of being**. Add the suffix –**ness** to each
word to make a new word. Then, write the new word.

1. wild_____   _____

2. soft_____   _____

3. swift_____   _____

4. mild_____   _____

5. cold_____   _____

Lesson 23 Words with ld and ft

Fun with Words

Antonyms are words that mean the opposite of other words. Write the spelling word that is an antonym of each word below.

1. slow   _____

2. bought   _____

3. right   _____

4. before   _____

5. dropped   _____

6. tame   _____

Words Across the Curriculum

Say each art word. Then, write the word.

1. gold   _____   3. craft   _____

2. mold   _____   4. tuft   _____

Write the art word that correctly completes each sentence.

1. You can _____ clay into many different shapes.

2. The color _____ contains yellow, green, and red.

3. You can tie the ends of yarn pieces into a knot to make a

_____.

4. Basket weaving is a _____ that is easy to learn.

Lesson 23 Words with ld and ft

Words in Writing
Write a summary of a movie that you saw or a book that you read. Use at least four words from the box.

| gift | left | held | wild | drift | gold | craft |
| sold | raft | swift | after | world | mold | tuft |

_____
_____
_____
_____
_____
_____
_____
_____

Dictionary Practice
Identify each word below as being most commonly used as a **noun**, **verb**, or **adjective**. Some words can be more than one part of speech. Use the dictionary in the back if you need help.

1. gift _____
2. wild _____
3. raft _____
4. held _____

5. swift _____
6. sold _____
7. world _____
8. drift _____

Lesson 24 Words with the /kw/ and /skw/ Sounds

Say each word. Listen to the beginning sound. Then, write the word.

Spelling Tips	The /kw/ sound is always spelled **qu**. The /skw/ sound is always spelled **squ**.

Spelling Words

quiet _____

quack _____

queen _____

squeeze _____

quilt _____

squeak _____

quick _____

squirrel _____

quite _____

question _____

Lesson 24 Words with the /kw/ and /skw/ Sounds

Words in Context
Write the missing spelling words.

Challenge

Circle the other words in the story with the /kw/ or /skw/ sounds.

Stella Finally Sleeps

Once, there was a _____

named Stella who ruled a small country. Stella was _____
happy with her life. She had only one worry: she couldn't sleep. Every night,

Stella got in her bed and covered herself with her favorite _____.

Stella would _____ her eyes shut and try to sleep.

Even if her room was perfectly _____, Stella imagined

that she heard queer sounds. Sometimes, she heard the _____

of a duck, the _____ of a mouse, or the squeal of a pig.

Other times, she heard a _____ crunching nuts with its teeth.
Once, she even heard the squirt of ink from a squid
swimming in the ocean.

When she heard these sounds, Stella would toss
and squirm in her bed. Stella did not quit trying

to answer the _____ of why
she kept hearing these sounds. Finally, she
solved her problem with a strange but

_____ solution. She started
wearing earplugs at night.

Lesson 24 Words with the /kw/ and /skw/ Sounds

Fun with Words

Write the spelling word that belongs with each pair of words.

1. silence, hush, _____

2. fast, swift, _____

3. princess, king, _____

4. blanket, cover, _____

5. command, exclamation, _____

6. very, greatly, _____

7. chirp, cluck, _____

8. chipmunk, groundhog, _____

Words Across the Curriculum

Say each math word. Then, write the word.

1. quart _____   3. quotient _____

2. quarter _____   4. quiz _____

Write the math word that completes each sentence.

1. One _____ equals twenty-five cents.

2. It's easy to get behind in math if you don't take a

   _____ every week.

3. Two pints equal one _____.

4. The answer to a division problem is called a _____.

Lesson 24 Words with the /kw/ and /skw/ Sounds

Words in Writing

Make up a fairy tale or a short story.
Use at least four words from the box.

quiet	queen	quilt	quick	quite	quart	quotient
quack	squeeze	squeak	squirrel	question	quarter	quiz

_____

_____

_____

_____

_____

_____

_____

Dictionary Practice

Write the correct symbol for the vowel sound
in the first or only syllable of each word.

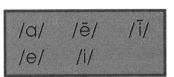

/a/   /ē/   /ī/
/e/   /i/

1. squeeze _____   5. quick _____

2. quack _____   6. squeak _____

3. quite _____   7. quiet _____

4. question _____   8. quilt _____

NAME _____

Lesson 25 Words with Silent **k** or Silent **w**

Say each word. Listen to the beginning sound. Notice that the beginning letter **k** or **w** is silent. Then, write the word.

Spelling Tips	The letter **k** is silent when followed by the letter **n**. The letter **w** is silent when followed by the letter **r**.

Spelling Words

know _____

wrist _____

knife _____

knob _____

wrong _____

knee _____

wrote _____

knock _____

wren _____

knight _____

Lesson 25 Words with Silent **k** or Silent **w**

Words in Context

Write the missing spelling words.

Sir Lancelot

A long time ago, a well-known writer

_____ an exciting story about a _____

named Lancelot. He was known as a very good man

who never did anything _____.
Lancelot had many adventures as he rode
around the country.

One time, Lancelot came to a castle
that seemed to be empty. As Lancelot began

to _____ on the door, the

_____ turned, and a lady opened
the door. She was crying because her pet falcon

had chased a small, brown _____ into

a tree and wouldn't come down. Lancelot put down

his sword and his _____. He took off his armor. Then, he
made a knot in a rope tied to his horse's saddle and wrapped the rope
around the tree. Lancelot climbed the tree and held out his arm to the

falcon. It jumped onto his _____. As Lancelot returned the

falcon to the lady, he bent one _____ and kneeled in front

of her. He didn't _____ that an enemy was hiding in some
bushes. That began another adventure.

Lesson 25 Words with Silent **k** or Silent **w**

Fun with Words

Write the spelling word that fits each clue.

1. You need me to help you open a door. _____

2. I am a man, but I'm covered with metal. _____

3. You have to bend me to walk. _____

4. I am never right. _____

5. I can make a signal when there's no doorbell. _____

6. I am a blade, but I'm not grass. _____

Words Across the Curriculum

Say each language arts word. Then, write the word.

1. written _____ 3. known _____

2. writing _____ 4. knew _____

Write the language arts word that completes each sentence.

1. _____ is a process that includes brainstorming, drafting, writing, editing, and proofreading.

2. More than 3,000 languages are _____ to exist in the world.

3. At one time, most people who spoke English _____ the stories of King Arthur and Sir Lancelot.

4. The legend of King Arthur and his knights was first _____ in the 1400s.

Lesson 25 Words with Silent **k** or Silent **w**

Words in Writing

Imagine that you are a knight who lived long ago.
Write a journal entry that tells what one of your days
might be like. Use at least four words from the box.

know	knife	wrong	wrote	wren	written	known
wrist	knob	knee	knock	knight	writing	knew

_____

_____

_____

_____

_____

_____

_____

_____

_____

Dictionary Practice

Write the word from the box that fits each pronunciation.

1. /nō/ _____

2. /rit´ ən/ _____

3. /nīt/ _____

4. /nē/ _____

5. /nok/ _____

6. /rīt´ ing/ _____

7. /rōt/ _____

8. /nīf/ _____

Lesson 26 Words with lf, mb, and tch

Say each word. Listen to the sounds **lf**, **mb**, and **tch**. Then, write the word.

Spelling Tips	In some words, the /f/ sound is spelled **lf**, the /m/ sound is spelled **mb**, and the /ch/ sound is spelled **tch**.

Spelling Words

half   _____

thumb   _____

match   _____

climb   _____

myself   _____

scratch   _____

pitcher   _____

shelf   _____

crumb   _____

kitchen   _____

Lesson 26 Words with lf, mb, and tch

Words in Context
Write the missing spelling words.

Making Cookies

I like to make cookies with my parents.

First, Dad switches on the oven. Then, I _____ up on a stool

to get the flour, sugar, and chocolate chips off the _____.
Next, Mom gets out the eggs and butter. I mix everything together by

_____, and then I shape the dough into balls. When the

balls are smooth, Mom slices them all in _____. She's careful

not to cut or _____ her fingers with the knife. I put the

pieces on a cookie sheet and flatten them with my _____.
Then, Dad puts all the pieces in the
oven and watches the clock for the
next fifteen minutes.

Soon, the _____
is filled with the wonderful smell of a
batch of warm cookies. Dad takes
them out of the oven and puts them

on a plate next to a _____
of milk. Everyone in my family agrees that warm cookies and cold milk are

a perfect _____. There won't be a single cookie

_____ left in a few hours.

Lesson 26 Words with **lf**, **mb**, and **tch**

Fun with Words

Write the spelling word that answers each question.

1. Where do you put a book? _____

2. What is each part of a pizza divided in two? _____

3. In what room is the food cooked in your home? _____

4. How do you get up a tree? _____

5. What do you do to an itch? _____

6. What is the smallest part of a cake left on a plate? _____

7. What would you use to light a candle? _____

8. What part of your hand is different from your fingers? _____

Words Across the Curriculum

Say each science word. Then, write the word.

1. lamb _____ 3. calf _____

2. hatch _____ 4. switch _____

Write the science word that completes each sentence.

1. A _____ is a baby cow.

2. Chicks _____ from eggs.

3. A _____ turns the light on and off.

4. A _____ grows up to be a sheep.

Lesson 26 Words with lf, mb, and tch

Words in Writing

What kind of snacks do you like to make?
Explain how you make a snack or meal.
Use at least four words from the box.

half	match	myself	pitcher	crumb	lamb	calf
thumb	climb	scratch	shelf	kitchen	hatch	switch

_____

_____

_____

_____

_____

Misspelled Words

Read the explanation. Circle the four misspelled words. Then, write the words correctly on the lines below.

   When I get home from school, I go into the kichen to make a snack. I usually make myself haf a sandwich. I cut a piece of bread in two. Then, I get some ham and cheese from a shelf in the refrigerator. I grab a picher of iced-tea, too. Once I put my sandwich together and pour my drink, my stomach is growling. I eat every crum.

_____   _____

_____   _____

Review Lessons 23–26

Write the spelling word that means the opposite.

1. before   _____

2. noisy   _____

3. whole   _____

4. answer   _____

5. tame   _____

6. bought   _____

Write the spelling word that fits each pair of words.

1. bedroom, dining room,   _____

2. chipmunk, rabbit,   _____

3. fork, spoon,   _____

4. himself, yourself   _____

5. king, princess,   _____

6. leg, ankle,   _____

7. blanket, cover,   _____

8. printed, typed   _____

Review Lessons 23–26

Write the spelling word that rhymes with each pair of words.

1. stack, back, _____

2. missed, kissed, _____

3. please, breeze, _____

4. so, row, _____

5. time, rhyme, _____

6. weld, spelled, _____

7. speak, leak, _____

8. long, song, _____

9. curled, twirled, _____

10. hen, then _____

Answer the following questions.

1. Which two spelling words mean **fast**?

   _____   _____

2. Which two spelling words rhyme with **fight**?

   _____   _____

3. Which two spelling words rhyme with **catch**?

   _____   _____

4. Which two spelling words rhyme with **drum**?

   _____   _____

Lesson 27 Words with the /âr/ Sound

Say each word. Listen to the /âr/ sound. Then, write the word.

Spelling Tips	The /âr/ sound can be spelled **air**, **are**, and **ear**.

Spelling Words

care　　　　　　_____

wear　　　　　　_____

share　　　　　　_____

bear　　　　　　_____

hair　　　　　　_____

pear　　　　　　_____

chair　　　　　　_____

fair　　　　　　_____

dare　　　　　　_____

stare　　　　　　_____

Lesson 27 Words with the /âr/ Sound

Words in Context

Write the missing spelling words.

Fun for Everyone

Are you aware that the state

_____ will be held next week? There will be all kinds of fun

things to _____ with your family and friends. Be sure to

_____ comfortable clothes, because
you will want to stay all day. There will
be some very exciting rides for

those who _____
to get on them. When you need
to rest from the glare of the sun,

you can sit in a _____
and listen to one of the bands.
    You won't want to miss the rare

black polar _____ and her pair of newborn cubs.

But beware! You must take _____ not to get too close to

their cage. If you see the _____ on the mother's neck rise,

and she starts to _____ at you, it's time to move on to the
farm building. There, you can see the largest apple, peach, and

_____ grown this summer.

Lesson 27 Words with the /âr/ Sound

Fun with Words

Write the spelling word that completes each sentence and is a homophone of the word in bold.

1. Will you please **pare** a _____ for me?

2. The cage of the _____ is **bare**.

3. What is the **fare** to ride the bus to the _____?

4. The **hare** has soft brown _____ on its ears.

5. **Where** will you _____ that hat?

6. Why did the girl _____ at the **stair**?

Words Across the Curriculum

Say each science word. Then, write the word.

1. air   _____   3. mare   _____

2. hare   _____   4. lair   _____

Write the science word that completes each sentence.

1. The _____ is in the field with her colt.

2. A _____ looks like a rabbit.

3. People breathe _____ into their lungs.

4. The wolf was hiding in its _____.

Lesson 27 Words with the /âr/ Sound

Words in Writing

What events or places do you like to go to? Write an ad about a place or event. Use at least four words from the box.

care	share	hair	chair	dare	air	mare
wear	bear	pear	fair	stare	hare	lair

_____

_____

_____

_____

_____

_____

Dictionary Practice

Look at each pair of guide words. Circle the word that comes between them in alphabetical order.

1. bear—bore	brake	black	bump
2. air—and	ask	ape	all
3. spare—sure	stare	snare	swan
4. chair—clear	cent	city	cost
5. slide—spoon	skip	share	smack
6. warm—when	wear	wisp	woven

Lesson 28 Words with the /ôr/ and /ûr/ Sounds

Say each word. Listen to the /ôr/ or /ûr/ sound. Then, write the word.

Spelling Tips	The /ôr/ sound can be spelled **or**, **oor**, and **ore**. The /ûr/ sound can be spelled **ir**, **or**, and **ur**.

Spelling Words

dirt   _____

order   _____

door   _____

worst   _____

hurt   _____

score   _____

before   _____

hurry   _____

sport   _____

nurse   _____

Lesson 28 Words with the /ôr/ and /ûr/ Sounds

Words in Context

Write the missing spelling words.

Ouch!

My last baseball game was the

_____ game of my life. In the ninth

inning, the _____ was tied 3-3. It was

my turn in the batting _____. I hit the

ball and saw an outfielder _____ toward the ball. I ran to first
base and was rounding the corner to second when I slipped and fell to

the _____. I knew right away that my ankle was badly

_____. I had never felt such pain _____ in my life.
My dad took me to the hospital and had to carry me through the

_____. A _____ took me in a room and asked
me some questions. Then, she took me to get an X-ray. Later, the doctor
told me that my ankle was sprained. I had to use crutches for two weeks.

Still, baseball is my favorite _____.

Word Building

The prefix **re-** means **to do again**. Add the prefix **re-** to each word to make
a new word. Then, write the word.

1. _____order _____
2. _____fill _____
3. _____pay _____
4. _____read _____
5. _____heat _____
6. _____start _____
7. _____write _____
8. _____view _____

Lesson 28 Words with the /ôr/ and /ûr/ Sounds

Fun with Words

Circle the hidden spelling words. Words can be across or down.

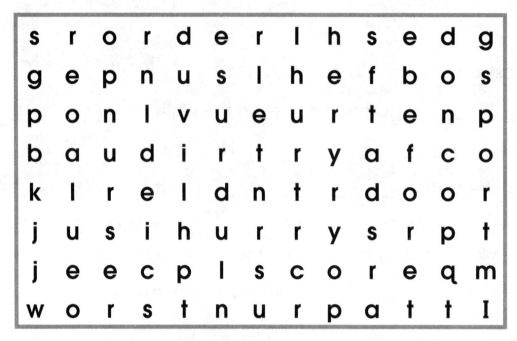

s	r	o	r	d	e	r	l	h	s	e	d	g
g	e	p	n	u	s	l	h	e	f	b	o	s
p	o	n	l	v	u	e	u	r	t	e	n	p
b	a	u	d	i	r	t	r	y	a	f	c	o
k	l	r	e	l	d	n	t	r	d	o	o	r
j	u	s	i	h	u	r	r	y	s	r	p	t
j	e	e	c	p	l	s	c	o	r	e	q	m
w	o	r	s	t	n	u	r	p	a	t	t	l

Words Across the Curriculum

Say each science word. Then, write the word.

1. fur   _____   3. herd   _____

2. storm   _____   4. forest   _____

Write the science word that completes each sentence.

1. A group of cows or sheep is called a _____.

2. A _____ has many trees.

3. Many mammals are covered with _____.

4. You might see lightning during a _____.

Lesson 28 Words with the /ôr/ and /ûr/ Sounds

Words in Writing

What sports do you like to play? Write a paragraph that tells about a time when you played the sport. Use at least four words from the box.

| dirt | door | hurt | before | sport | fur | herd |
| order | worst | score | hurry | nurse | storm | forest |

_____

_____

_____

_____

_____

_____

Misspelled Words

Read the paragraph. Circle the four misspelled words. Then, write the words correctly on the lines below.

Soccer is my favorite sporte. My team had a game last Monday. We practiced for a little while befor the game. As I was trying to scor a goal, I fell down and scraped my knees in the durt. It didn't really hurt, though. I got to play the whole game.

_____   _____

_____   _____

Lesson 29 Compound Words

Say each word. Listen to the two words that make up the compound word. Then, write the word.

Spelling Tip	Compound words are made by putting two smaller words together.

Spelling Words

popcorn   _____

cookout   _____

sailboat   _____

seashell   _____

barefoot   _____

birthday   _____

moonlight   _____

airplane   _____

sandcastle   _____

everything   _____

Lesson 29 Compound Words

Words in Context
Write the missing spelling words.

A Great Weekend Trip

Challenge

Circle the other compound words in the journal entry.

My _____ was last

Saturday, so my grandparents took me on a weekend trip to the beach.

We flew on an _____ to get there. When we got to our

beach house, we walked _____ on the sand. We also

made a _____ and waded in the ocean. I found a smooth,

white _____.

Later in the afternoon, we floated on the ocean

in a _____. Afterward, we had a

_____ with cheeseburgers and _____. I fed some

crumbs to a seagull. In the evening, we walked along the seashore in the

_____. _____ about that day was wonderful.

Word Building
Add one of the smaller words from a spelling word to each word below to make a new compound word. Then, write the new compound word.

1. _____ shore   _____

2. _____ box   _____

3. _____ ball   _____

4. sun _____   _____

5. _____ book   _____

Lesson 29 Compound Words

Fun with Words

Combine the two words in each sentence that make a compound spelling word.

1. Look at the castle made of sand.   _____

2. Can you see the pale light of the moon?   _____

3. The corn soon began to pop loudly.   _____

4. When do you celebrate the day of your birth?   _____

5. My foot was bare when I took off my sandal.   _____

6. Do you like to sail on a boat?   _____

7. Look at this shell that I found by the sea.   _____

8. Come out so we can cook some hot dogs
   on the grill.   _____

Words Across the Curriculum

Say each science word. Then, write the word.

1. eardrum _____   3. snowflake _____

2. rainbow _____   4. backbone _____

Write the science word that completes each sentence.

1. A _____ is made of tiny ice crystals.

2. Another name for an animals' spine is a _____.

3. The _____ allows a person to hear sounds.

4. Water drops in the sky reflect light to make a _____.

Lesson 29 Compound Words

Words in Writing

What places in nature do you like? Write a description of a natural habitat you like to visit. Use at least four words from the box.

| popcorn | sailboat | barefoot | moonlight | sandcastle | eardrum | rainbow |
| cookout | seashell | birthday | airplane | everything | snowflake | backbone |

_____

_____

_____

_____

_____

_____

Dictionary Practice

Write the words from the box that belong in each column. Some words belong in two columns.

/ā/	/ē/	/ō/
_____	_____	_____
_____	_____	_____
_____		_____
_____		_____
_____		

Lesson 30 More Compound Words

Say each word. Listen to the two words that make up the compound word. Then, write the word.

Spelling Tip	Compound words are made by putting two smaller words together.

Spelling Words

hallway   _____

sidewalk   _____

farmhouse   _____

hillside   _____

inside   _____

springtime   _____

driveway   _____

cornfield   _____

downstairs   _____

horseback   _____

Lesson 30 More Compound Words

Words in Context
Write the missing spelling words.

For Sale

Challenge

Circle the other compound words in the description.

There is an old _____ for

sale. The house was built on a _____. The front yard has two

rows of tall trees leading from the _____ to the house. It also

has a flowerbed that is filled with colorful tulips in the _____.

A long _____ leads behind the house to the garage. Behind

the backyard is a large _____
with stalks that grow six feet tall in the
summer. There is a trail around the field

where people can ride on _____.

The rooms _____ the house are very nice. The kitchen,

living room, and dining room are _____. Upstairs, the

bedrooms and bathroom are all connected by a long _____.
This house will make a good home for anyone who buys it.

Word Building
Add one of the smaller words from a spelling word to each word below to make a new compound word.

1. _____town   _____

2. any_____   _____

3. _____pack   _____

Lesson 30 More Compound Words

Fun with Words

Combine the words in the box to make eight spelling words.

| back | down | farm | hall | house | stairs | walk |
| corn | drive | field | horse | spring | time | way |

1. _____   5. _____

2. _____   6. _____

3. _____   7. _____

4. _____   8. _____

Words Across the Curriculum

Say each social studies word. Then, write the word.

1. railroad _____   3. firefighter_____

2. stoplight _____   4. crosswalk_____

Write each social studies word next to its definition.

1. a light that signals for car drivers to stop   _____

2. a track that trains run on   _____

3. a person who puts out fires   _____

4. a place where people walk across a street   _____

Lesson 30 More Compound Words

Words in Writing

Write a description of where you live.
Use at least four words from the box.

hallway	farmhouse	inside	driveway	downstairs	railroad	stoplight
sidewalk	hillside	springtime	cornfield	horseback	firefighter	crosswalk

_____

_____

_____

_____

_____

_____

_____

Misspelled Words

Read the description. Circle the five misspelled words. Then, write the words correctly on the lines below.

   My house is in the country near a railrode track. There are only a few houses on my street, so it doesn't have a sidewak. We live next to a farmhouse that has a big cornfeld behind it. When the snow melts in the sprigtime, I get to ride in the field on horsback.

_____   _____   _____

_____   _____

Review Lessons 27–30

Write the spelling word that is a homophone of each word below.

1. bare _____

2. fare _____

3. stair _____

4. where _____

5. pair _____

6. hare _____

Write the spelling word that belongs with each word.

1. doctor and _____

2. table and _____

3. window and _____

4. law and _____

5. truth or _____

6. game and _____

7. _____ and after

8. best and _____

Review Lessons 27–30

Write the compound spelling word that fits each clue.

1. This season follows wintertime.   _____

2. You might see this in the sky at night.   _____

3. You have no shoes on.   _____

4. You might see a scarecrow in this.   _____

5. Cars are sometimes parked here.   _____

6. This is the day you were born.   _____

7. You can ride on water in this.   _____

8. This is a snack that goes with movies.   _____

9. You walk along a street on this.   _____

10. You are not outside.   _____

11. You can make this on a beach.   _____

12. You can fly in the air in this.   _____

13. This is the lower level of a house.   _____

14. You can sled down this in the winter.   _____

15. You walk down this to get to your classroom. _____

16. You can travel this way on a ranch.   _____

A

a·bout *prep.* Pertaining to. *adv.* Not exactly.

a·cross *prep.* On the other side of; from one side to another.

af·ter *prep.* Following.

af·ter·noon *n.* The time between 12 o'clock noon and about 5 p.m.

a·gain *adv.* Once more.

air *n.* The sky; the mixture of gasses that surrounds the Earth.

air·plane *n.* An engine-powered vehicle capable of flight.

al·low *v.* To let or permit.

a·lone *adj.* or *adv.* Away from other people; by oneself.

al·ways *adv.* Forever; at all times.

a·mount *n.* Total quantity; sum.

an·noy *v.* To bother; to irritate.

A·pril *n.* The fourth month of the calendar year.

ar·e·a *n.* The product of length and width.

August *n.* The eighth month of the calendar year.

au·tumn *n.* The season between summer and winter; the fall.

a·void *v.* To stay away from.

a·wake *v.* To wake up.

a·way *adv.* At a distance.

B

back·bone *n.* The spine of an animal.

baked *adj.* Cooked in an oven.

bare·foot *adj.* and *adv.* Having nothing on the feet.

bath *n.* The act of washing the body.

bat·tle *n.* Combat between opposing forces *v.* To engage in a war.

bear *n.* A large mammal with shaggy fur and short tail.

be·cause *conj.* For a reason.

be·fore *adv.* Earlier. *prep.* In front of.

ber·ries *n.* Pieces of fruit that can be eaten.

ber·ry *n.* Fruit that can be eaten.

bet·ter *adj.* Of higher quality; more useful.

be·tween *prep.* In the middle; shared by two.

birth·day *n.* The day a person is born and the anniversary of that day.

boi·ling *v.* A liquid forming bubbles that escape as steam because of heating.

bot·tle *n.* A container used to hold liquid.

bus·y *adj.* Full of activity.

buzz *v.* To make a low, vibrating humming sound, like a bee.

C

cal·en·dar *n.* A system for showing time divisions by years, months, weeks, and days.

calf *n.* A young cow.

care *n.* A feeling of concern. *v.* To show interest.

cas·tle *n.* A fort or strong building for nobility.

cat·tle *pl. n.* Farm animals raised for meat and dairy products.

caught *v.* Past tense of catch. Captured or grasped; trapped.

cell *n.* The smallest unit of any organism.

cent *n.* A penny.

cen·ter *n.* The place of equal distance from all sides.

chair *n.* A seat with four legs and a back.

chalk *n.* A soft mineral used for marking on a surface, such as a slate board.

chill *v.* To make cold. *n.* A feeling of cold.

choice *n.* Selection.

chose *v.* Past tense of choose. Selected or picked.

Christ·mas *n.* December 25, a Christian holiday celebrating the birth of Jesus.

cir·cle *n.* A curved form that ends at its starting point; in the shape of a wheel.

cit·ies *n.* Plural form of city. Communities of homes and businesses.

cit·y *n.* A community of homes and businesses.

cliff *n.* A high, steep edge of a rock.

climb *v.* To move to a higher or lower location.

cloud *n.* A visible body of water droplets or ice particles floating in the sky.

clue *n.* A hint.

coach *n.* A trainer or director of athletics, drama, or other skill.

Co·lum·bus Day *n.* October 12, a holiday celebrating Christopher Columbus's discovery of the Americas.

cook·out *n.* A gathering of people with the meal grilled outside.

cool *adj.* Chilly temperature.

corn·field *n.* A field for growing corn.

craft *n.* An ability that requires artistic skill.

cray·on *n.* A stick of colored wax used for writing or drawing.

cre·at·ing *v.* Making; bringing something into existence.

cross·walk *n.* A path on a road marked for pedestrians.

crumb *n.* A small piece of material, especially food.

cy·cle *n.* A series of events that happen over and over again.

D

damp *adj.* Slightly wet.

dare *v.* To show courage; to try something.

dawn *n.* The beginning of a new day.

De·cem·ber *n.* The twelfth month of the calendar year.

dew *n.* Early morning moisture from the sky.

din·ner *n.* The main meal of the day, usually eaten in the evening.

dirt *n.* Soil or earth.

div·ing *v.* Jumping into water headfirst.

dol·lar *n.* A unit of money equal to 100 cents.

done *adj.* Completely finished.

door *n.* A swinging panel used to go in or out of a building.

down·stairs *n.* The lower floor.

draw *v.* To sketch.

drift *v.* To be carried along by currents of water or air.

drive·way *n.* A road leading to a house or garage.

dune *n.* A hill of sand.

E

ea·gle *n.* A large bird of prey.

ear·drum *n.* The part of the ear that receives sounds.

ear·ly *adj.* Occurring near the beginning of a period of time.

eas·y *adj.* Simple.

edge *n.* A side of a geometric figure; the sharp side of a blade; the cliff of a mountain.

else *adv.* If not; otherwise.

en·joy *v.* To find happiness in something.

e·qual *adj.* Of the same quantity or value as another.

e·rase *v.* To remove something written.

eve·ning *n.* The time between sunset and bedtime.

eve·ry·thing *pron.* All things.

F

fact *n.* Something that actually occurred or exists.

fail *v.* To be unsuccessful.

fair *n.* A gathering of people to show goods and enjoy entertainment.

fall *n.* Autumn.

farm·house *n.* A home on a farm.

Fa·ther's Day *n.* The third Sunday in June, a holiday celebrating fathers.

fa·vor·ite *n.* Anything liked above all others.

Feb·ru·ar·y *n.* The second month of the calendar year.

fence *n.* A wall used to mark off an area outside.

fill *v.* To supply as much of something as can be contained.

finish *v.* To end or complete.

fired *v.* Past tense of fire. Made firm by heating in a oven.

fire·fight·er *n.* A person who fights fires.

flap *n.* A piece of material that can move because it is attached on only one side. *v.* To move up and down.

flock *n.* A group of animals of all the same kind, especially birds.

flow·er *n.* The part of a plant that has colorful petals.

for·est *n.* A large area of land covered with trees.

Fri·day *n.* The sixth day of a calendar week.

frost *n.* A covering of small ice crystals on a cold surface.

frown *v.* To lower the ends of the lips as in anger, sadness, or displeasure.

fur *n.* The hairy covering of an animal.

fu·ture *n.* The time to come.

G

gal·lon *n.* A liquid measurement equal to 4 quarts.

gen·er·al *n.* The leader of an army.

gi·ant *adj.* Having great size.

gift *n.* Something given from one person to another.

glazed *v.* Past tense of glaze. Covered with a thin, smooth coating, as on pottery.

gloss *n.* The brightness of a polished surface.

goal *n.* A purpose; a score during a sport.

gold *n.* A yellow color.

great·er *adj.* More than something else.

grew *v.* Past tense of grow. Increased in size and maturity.

grill *v.* To cook on an object that uses an open flame.

guess *v.* To form an opinion based on incomplete knowledge.

gym *n.* A room or building used for indoor sports

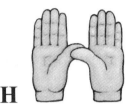

H

hair *n.* Fine, threadlike growths on the skin of human beings and other mammals.

half *n.* One of two equal parts.

Hal·low·een *n.* October 31, a holiday celebrated by children dressed in costumes and going to houses for candy or pranks.

hall·way *n.* A passage that leads to rooms in a house.

ham·mer *n.* A hand tool with a heavy head used to hit nails.

Ha·nuk·kah *n.* The eight-day Jewish holiday celebrating the rededication of the Temple in Jerusalem.

hap·pen *v.* To take place or occur.

hare *n.* A mammal related to a rabbit but with longer ears and legs.

hatch *v.* To be born from an egg.

hav·ing *v.* Owning or being in possession of.

he'd *contr.* The short form of *he would* or *he had*.

head *n.* The upper part of a body, containing the brain.

held *v.* Past tense of hold. Kept, hung on to.

herd *n.* A group of animals of the same kind.

hid·ing *v.* Keeping out of sight.

high *adj.* Located some distance above the ground.

hiked *v.* Past tense of hike. Went on a long walk.

hill·side *n.* The side of a hill.

his·to·ry *n.* Past events.

hob·by *n.* An activity done for fun.

hoped *v.* Past tense of hope. Wanted or wished for something.

horse·back *adj.* and *adv.* On the back of a horse.

hun·dred *n.* The number equal to 10 x 10.

hur·ry *v.* To move quickly; to rush.

hurt *v.* To experience pain.

I

I'd *contr.* Short form of *I would* and *I had*.

In·de·pen·dence Day *n.* July 4, a holiday celebrating the signing of the Declaration of Independence and the birth of the United States.

in·side *n.* The space that is within.

it'll *contr.* Short form for *it will* and *it shall*.

I've *contr.* Short form of *I have*.

J

jack·et *n.* A light coat.

Jan·u·ar·y *n.* The first month of the calendar year.

join *v.* To bring together.

joke *n.* Something said or done to cause laughter.

jour·ney *n.* A trip from one place to another.

judge *n.* A person who passes judgment in a court. *v.* To decide or settle.

juice *n.* The liquid part of a vegetable or fruit.

Ju·ly *n.* The seventh month of the calendar year.

June *n.* The sixth month of the calendar year.

jun·gle *n.* Land with tropical plants, usually inhabited by wild animals.

K

kitch·en *n.* A room used to cook food.

knee *n.* The joint in the leg connecting the calf with the thigh.

knew *v.* Past tense of know. Understood clearly.

knife *n.* A tool used to cut.

knight *n.* A medieval soldier.

knob *n.* A round handle used to open a door.

knock *v.* To hit with a hard blow.

knot *n.* A fastening made by tying together lengths of string.

know *v.* To understand.

known *adj.* Widely understood.

L

La·bor Day *n.* The first Monday in September, a holiday celebrating working people.

lad·der *n.* A tool used for climbing up or down.

la·dies *n.* Plural of lady. Women.

la·dy *n.* A woman.

lair *n.* The home of a wild animal.

lamb *n.* A young sheep.

large *adj.* Big.

lat·er *adj.* Happening after the usual or current time.

lawn *n.* An area of ground covered with grass.

learn *v.* To gain knowledge.

left *adj.* The side of the body that faces north when facing east. *v.* Past tense of leave. Went away.

let·ter *n.* A note or written means of communication sent to another person.

lift *v.* To raise from a lower to a higher position.

lit·ter *n.* Trash.

live *v.* To exist.

lo·cate *v.* To determine the place of.

lose *v.* To fail to keep; to be beaten in a competition.

lots *adj.* Many.

loy·al *adj.* Faithful.

luck·y *adj.* Having good fortune.

M

mag·ic *n.* The skill of doing tricks that other people can not figure out.

mak·ing *v.* Creating.

mam·mal *n.* Any animal whose females produce milk for nourishing their young.

ma·ple *n.* A tree.

March *n.* The third month of the calendar year.

mare *n.* A female horse.

Mar·tin Lu·ther King Day *n.* The third Monday in January, a holiday celebrating Martin Luther King, Jr.

mass *n.* The amount of matter that an object has.

match *n.* Anything that is similar or identical to another; a small piece of wood used to start a fire.

mat·ter *n.* Something that makes up the substance of anything.

May *n.* The fifth month of the calendar year.

Me·mo·ri·al Day *n.* May 30, a holiday remembering those in the armed forces killed in battle.

mid·dle *adj.* Being in the center.

might *v.* Used to ask permission or express possibility.

mile *n.* A unit of measurement equaling 5,280 feet.

min·ute *n.* The unit of time equaling 60 seconds.

miss *v.* To fail to hit, reach, or make contact with something.

mold *v.* To shape into a form.

Mon·day *n.* The second day of a calendar week.

mood *n.* A state of mind or feeling.

moon·light *n.* The light of the moon.

morn·ing *n.* The early part of the day; the time from midnight to noon.

most *adj.* The majority of. *n.* The greatest amount.

Moth·er's Day *n.* The second Sunday of May, celebrating mothers.

mouth *n.* The bodily opening through which food is taken in.

move *v.* To set in motion.

my·self *pron.* The one who is me.

N

nev·er *adv.* At no time, not ever.

New Year's Day *n.* January 1, a holiday celebrating the first day of a new year.

nick·el *n.* A coin worth five cents.

noise *n.* A loud sound.

noon *n.* The middle of the day; 12:00 o'clock.

not *adv.* Used to express refusal or denial.

No·vem·ber *n.* The eleventh month of the calendar year.

nurse *n.* A person trained to care for sick persons.

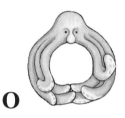

O

Oc·to·ber *n.* The tenth month of the calendar year.

odd *adj.* Not evenly divided by two; strange.

or·der *n.* A logical arrangement of things.

oth·er *adj.* Additional. *pron.* A different person or thing.

ounce *n.* A unit of weight that equals 1/16 of a pound.

oys·ter *n.* An ocean animal that is enclosed in a shell.

P

page *n.* One side of the leaf of a book or letter.

pair *n.* Two things that are similar and go together.

par·ties *n.* Plural of party. Groups of people who get together for fun or entertainment.

par·ty *n.* A group of persons who gather for fun or entertainment.

pat·tern *n.* An arrangement of colors, shapes, or lines.

paw *n.* The foot of an animal.

peace *n.* A state of calmness.

pear *n.* A juicy fruit.

peb·ble *n.* A small, smooth stone.

pen·cil *n.* A tool for writing or drawing.

pen·nies *pl. n.* Plural of penny. Cents.

pen·ny *n.* A coin worth one cent.

pic·ture *n.* An image of something.

piece *n.* A part of a whole.

pitch·er *n.* The person who throws a baseball to the batter; a container for holding and pouring liquids.

place *n.* An area.

pock·et *n.* A small pouch in clothes used for carrying items.

point *n.* The sharp end of something.

poi·son *n.* A substance that kills or injures..

po·lice *n.* A department organized to maintain law and order.

pol·lute *v.* To make dirty.

po·nies *pl. n.* Plural of pony. Small horses.

po·ny *n.* A small horse.

pop·corn *n.* A type of corn that, when heated, forms white puffs.

pound *n.* A measure of weight equal to sixteen ounces.

puff *n.* A brief discharge of air or smoke.

pul·ley *n.* A wheel used with a rope to lift objects.

pup·pies *n.* Plural of puppy. Young dogs.

pup·py *n.* A young dog.

Q

quack *n.* The croaking sound made by a duck.

quart *n.* A unit of measurement equal to four cups.

quar·ter *n.* A coin equal to twenty-five cents.

queen *n.* A royal woman who rules a country.

ques·tion *n.* An expression of asking.

quick *adj.* Fast.

qui·et *adj.* Silent.

quilt *n.* A blanket sewn in a decorative design.

quiz *n.* An informal test.

quo·tient *n.* In math, the number that results when one number is divided by another.

R

raft *n.* A floating structure made from logs or planks.

rab·bit *n.* A small animal with long ears that moves by hopping.

rail·road *n.* The track that a train travels on.

rain·bow *n.* An arc in the sky containing bands of colors.

raise *v.* To cause to move upward.

Ram·a·dan *n.* The ninth month of the year in the Islamic calendar; the holiest period of time for Islam.

range *n.* The limits of.

rat·tle *n.* A series of quick, sharp noises. *v.* To make a series of quick, sharp noises.

read·y *adj.* Prepared for use or action.

re·lig·ion *n.* An organized system of beliefs.

rice *n.* The grains of a cereal grass grown for food.

rid·ing *v.* Traveling in a vehicle or on an animal.

right *adj.* Correct, right, or proper. *n.* The right side, hand, or direction; the direction opposite left.

rip·ple *n.* A small wave on the surface of liquid or cloth. *v.* To form small waves on the surface of water.

root *n.* The part of a plant that grows in the ground.

round *adj.* Curved; circular; spherical. *v.* To make an approximate number.

rule *n.* A law or diction meant to be followed. *v.* To govern or control.

S

sad·dle *n.* A seat for a rider, as on the back of a horse or bicycle.

sail·boat *n.* A boat that moves by wind in a sail.

sand·cast·le *n.* A castle made from sand.

Sat·ur·day *n.* The seventh day of a calendar week.

sauce *n.* A liquid or dressing served with or on food.

scale *n.* The ratio that a map or model has to the place or that that it represents; a device for weighing.

school *n.* A place for teaching and learning.

sci·ence *n.* The study and explanation of natural phenomena.

scoop *n.* A small, shovel-like tool. *v.* To lift up or out.

score *n.* A numerical record of total points won in a game.

scratch *n.* A small scrape or cut. *v.* To mark or make a slight cut on; to dig with claws or nails.

sea·shell *n.* A shell from or found in the sea.

sea·son *n.* One of the four parts of the year: spring, summer, fall or autumn, and winter.

sense *n.* Any of the ways that living things can observe objects (sight, hearing, smell, taste, and touch); feeling.

Sep·tem·ber *n.* The ninth month of the calendar year.

set·tle *v.* To colonize; to restore calm to.

sew *v.* To make stitches with thread and needle.

shap·ing *v.* Giving something form.

share *n.* A part or portion given to or by one person. *v.* To use or take part in together with others.

shelf *n.* A flat piece of material used to hold or store things.

she'll *contr.* Short form of *she will* and *she shall*.

shin·ing *v.* Giving off light.

should·n't *contr.* Short form of should not.

shout *n.* A loud cry. *v.* To yell.

show·er *n.* A short period of rain; a bath with water spraying down on the bather.

side·walk *n.* A type of paved walk at the side of the street.

si·lence *n.* Quiet.

since *adv.* At a time before the present.

sin·gle *adj.* Of or referring to only one.

skat·ed *v.* Past tense of skate. Moved on skates.

smell *n.* An odor. *v.* To notice an odor.

smile *n.* A grin or expression of happiness made with the mouth.

snow·flake *n.* A small crystal of snow.

so *adv.* For a reason; to such a degree; also.

soc·cer *n.* A game in which two teams of eleven each try to kick a ball into the opposing team's goal.

soil *n.* Dirt; earth.

sold *v.* Past tense of sell. Exchanged for money.

sphere *n.* A round object; a globe.

spice *n.* A plant used as flavoring in food.

spill *v.* To cause something to flow or run out of a container.

splash *v.* To spatter a liquid.

split *v.* To divide or separate.

spoil *v.* To destroy the value, quality, or usefulness of something.

sport *n.* A game or physical activity with set rules.

spray *n.* A liquid in the form of a fine mist or droplets. *v.* To scatter liquid.

spread *n.* A cloth covering for a bed; soft food used to cover bread or other solid food. *v.* To unfold or open fully; to cover with a thin layer of something.

spring *n.* One of the four yearly seasons; a spiral-shaped piece of metal. *v.* To move forward quickly; to grow quickly.

spring·time *n.* The time of spring.

sprin·kle *v.* To drop little pieces over something.

sprout *n.* A plant just beginning to grow. *v.* To begin to grow.

square *n.* An object with four equal sides.

squeak *n.* A sharp sound. *v.* To utter a sharp sound.

squeeze *v.* To press together.

squir·rel *n.* A rodent with gray or brown fur and a fluffy tail.

stage *n.* A tall platform for plays or concerts.

stalk *n.* The main stem of a plant; a supporting part. *v.* To follow quietly.

stare *v.* To look at with a direct gaze.

stop·light *n.* A road light that controls traffic movements.

storm *n.* Weather marked by strong winds with rain, sleet, hail, or snow.

straight *adj.* Being without bends.

strange *adj.* Odd.

straw *n.* A stalk of dried grain.

stream *n.* A small body of flowing water.

street *n.* A road.

strip *n.* A long, narrow piece of something. *v.* To take off the outer covering.

stripe *n.* A streak, band, or strip of a different color or texture.

strong *adj.* Exerting or having physical power.

strum *v.* To play a stringed instrument by stroking fingers over the strings.

stuff *n.* Unnamed things. *v.* To pack full.

sum·mer *n.* The warmest of the four seasons.

Sun·day *n.* The first day of a calendar week.

swift *adj.* Moving with great speed.

switch *n.* A device for opening or closing an electric circuit. *v.* To exchange.

T

talk *v.* To communicate by words.

than *conj.* In comparison with or to something.

Thanks·giv·ing Day *n.* The fourth Thursday in November, a holiday celebrating the feast between pilgrims and Native Americans.

thaw *v.* To change from a frozen state to a liquid state.

they'd *contr.* Short form of they would and they had.

they'll *contr.* Short form of they will and they shall.

thou·sand *n.* The number equal to 10 x 100.

thumb *n.* The short first digit of the hand.

Thurs·day *n.* The fifth day of a calendar week.

tow·er *n.* A very tall building or structure.

trash *n.* Useless material thrown away.

tri·an·gle *n.* A figure with three sides and three angles.

true *adj.* Known to be correct.

Tues·day *n.* The third day of a calendar week.

tuft *n.* A small cluster of hair, thread, or other like material.

tur·tle *n.* A scaly-skinned animal having a soft body covered with a hard shell.

twice *adv.* Double; two times.

U

un·less *conj.* Except because of something else.

V

Val·en·tine's Day *n.* February 14, celebrating love.

vis·it *v.* To journey to or go to see a person or place.

voice *n.* The sound created by the mouth and throat.

vote *n.* The expression of one's choice by voice, by raising one's hand, or by secret ballot.

W

wage *n.* A payment of money for work or services.

wear *v.* To have on or put something on the body.

Wednes·day *n.* The fourth day of a calendar week.

well *n.* A hole in the ground that contains a supply of water. *adj.* Done in a good way; being in good health.

weren't *contr.* Short form of *were not.*

we've *contr.* Short form of *we have.*

wheel *n.* A circular disk that turns on an axle.

whole *adj.* Complete; having nothing missing.

wild *adj.* Living in a natural, untamed state.

win·ter *n.* The coldest season.

wipe *v.* To clean by rubbing.

wood *n.* The hard substance that makes up the main part of trees.

work *n.* The action or labor required to accomplish something.

world *n.* The planet Earth.

worst *adj.* Bad; most inferior.

would *v.* Past tense of will. Used to express a condition or hope.

would·n't *contr.* Short form of would not.

wren *n.* A small, brown songbird.

wrist *n.* The joint of the body between the hand and forearm.

write *v.* To form symbols or words on a surface.

writ·ing *v.* Forming symbols or words on a surface.

writ·ten *v.* Formed by symbols words on a surface.

wrong *adj.* Incorrect.

wrote *v.* Past tense of write. Formed symbols or words on a surface.

Y

you'd *contr.* Short form of *you would* and *you had*.

you'll *contr.* Short form of *you will* and *you shall*.

you're *contr.* Short form of *you are*.

Z

zip·per *n.* A fastener consisting of two rows of plastic or metal teeth.

Parts of Speech

adj. = adjective
adv. = adverb
art. = article
conj. = conjunction
n. = noun
prep. = preposition
pron. = pronoun
v. = verb

Answer Key

Say each word. Listen for the short **a** sound or the short **o** sound. Then, write the word.

Spelling Tips	The short **a** sound can be spelled **a**. The symbol for the short **a** sound is /a/. The short **o** sound can be spelled **o**. The symbol for the short **o** sound is /o/.

Spelling Words

bath	bath
hobby	hobby
than	than
damp	damp
bottle	bottle
lots	lots
trash	trash
flock	flock
pocket	pocket
flap	flap

6

Words in Context
Write the missing spelling words.

Science Is Everywhere

Challenge
Circle the other words in the narrative that have the /a/ or /o/ sound.

I like science more ____than____ any other subject at school. Science is also my ____hobby____. I always keep a pen and a notebook in my ____pocket____ to record things that I see.

Today, I went to the recycling center. I watched as old pieces of glass that once were ____trash____ were made into a new ____bottle____. After that, I walked along the river. I noticed ____lots____ of patches of soft, green moss growing in the ____damp____ soil. I watched a ____flock____ of birds looking for worms in the ground. A few birds waded into the river and started to ____flap____ their wings against the water. The birds were taking a ____bath____ as many other animals do.

Word Building
A flock is a group of birds. Write the word from the box that describes each group of animals.

pack	swarm	colony	school
pod	gaggle	herd	bed

1. a ____herd____ of cows   5. a ____school____ of fish
2. a ____pod____ of whales   6. a ____swarm____ of bees
3. a ____colony____ of ants   7. a ____pack____ of wolves
4. a ____gaggle____ of geese   8. a ____bed____ of clams

7

Fun with Words
Write the spelling word that completes each sentence and rhymes with the word in **bold**.

1. Sometimes, the ground is ____damp____ at **camp**.
2. A ____flock____ of crows landed on the **rock**.
3. I have a toy **rocket** in my ____pocket____.
4. You can get **cash** if you recycle your ____trash____.
5. When I finished my **math**, I took a warm ____bath____.
6. There are ____lots____ of **cots** in the cabin.
7. I closed the tent ____flap____ and lay down to take a **nap**.

Words Across the Curriculum
Say each math word. Then, write the word.

1. odd ____odd____   3. fact ____fact____
2. gallon ____gallon____   4. pattern ____pattern____

Write the math word that completes each sentence.

1. There are four quarts in one ____gallon____.
2. An example of an addition ____fact____ is 7 + 3 = 10.
3. A number that is ____odd____ can't be divided by 2.
4. The next number in the ____pattern____ 3, 6, 9 is 12.

8

Words in Writing
Write some notes about something you have found outside. Use at least four words from the box.

bath	than	bottle	trash	pocket	odd	fact
hobby	damp	lots	flock	flap	gallon	pattern

Answers will vary.

Misspelled Words
Read the recorded notes. Circle the four misspelled words. Then, write the words correctly on the lines below.

I found some moss growing on a tree trunk. It felt odd when I touched it. It was domp and softer then most plants. I took my hand lens from my poket and looked carefully at the small, flat plant. I could see a patten of lots of tiny green threads.

damp	pocket
than	pattern

9

Answer Key

Say each word. Listen for the short **e**, short **i**, or short **u** sound. Then, write the word.

Spelling Tips	The short **e** sound can be spelled **e** or **ea**. The symbol for the short **e** sound is /e/. The short **i** sound can be spelled **i**. The symbol for the short **i** sound is /i/. The short **u** sound can be spelled **u**. The symbol for the short **u** sound is /u/.

Spelling Words

else	else
buzz	buzz
finish	finish
head	head
summer	summer
lift	lift
ready	ready
visit	visit
fence	fence
live	live

10

Words in Context
Write the missing spelling words.

Challenge
Circle the other words in the article that have the /e/, /i/, or /u/ sound.

Track Meet

Now that ___summer___ is here, it's time for the final track meet. Students from other schools ___visit___ our school to run with us. Many other people who ___live___ in our city come too. They take their seats behind the ___fence___ next to the track. They come early, or ___else___ they have to stand. You can hear the ___buzz___ of the crowd as the runners get ___ready___ for the race. As the race officials ___lift___ their flags into the air, the crowd becomes silent. Every ___head___ is turned toward the runners. The flags go down, and they're off! All the people hold their breath until the runners cross the ___finish___ line.

11

Fun with Words
Unscramble the letters to make the spelling words.

1. veli ___live___   5. sele ___else___
2. ahed ___head___   6. deyar ___ready___
3. shifin ___finish___   7. muserm ___summer___
4. tilf ___lift___   8. efcen ___fence___

Words Across the Curriculum
Say each math word. Then, write the word.

1. edge ___edge___   3. nickel ___nickel___
2. hundred ___hundred___   4. minute ___minute___

Write the math word that completes each pattern.

1. ten, ___hundred___, thousand
2. angle, ___edge___, face
3. second, ___minute___, hour
4. penny, ___nickel___, dime

12

Words in Writing
Write a newspaper article that tells about a sports event. Use at least four words from the box.

| else | finish | summer | ready | fence | edge | nickel |
| buzz | head | lift | visit | live | hundred | minute |

Answers will vary.

Dictionary Practice
Each list of words begins with the same letter. Circle the second letter in each word. Then, number the words from 1–4 in alphabetical order.

1.
   - 3 finish
   - 4 flap
   - 2 fence
   - 1 fall

2.
   - 3 else
   - 2 eel
   - 1 edge
   - 4 end

3.
   - 4 hundred
   - 2 hide
   - 3 hold
   - 1 head

13

Answer Key

Page 14

Say each word. Listen for the long **a** or the long **o** sound. Then, write the word.

Spelling Tips	The long **a** sound can be spelled **a-consonant-e, ai,** or **ay**. The symbol for the long **a** sound is /ā/. The long **o** sound can be spelled **o, o-consonant-e,** or **oa**. The symbol for the long **o** sound is /ō/.

Spelling Words

goal	goal
fail	fail
away	away
most	most
alone	alone
awake	awake
chose	chose
crayon	crayon
coach	coach
raise	raise

14

Page 15

Words in Context
Write the missing spelling words.

A New Start

Challenge
Circle the other words in the article that have the /ā/ or /ō/ sound.

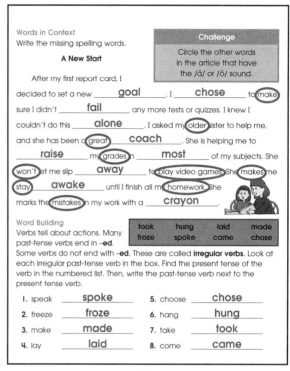

After my first report card, I decided to set a new **goal**. I **chose** to (make) sure I didn't **fail** any more tests or quizzes. I knew I couldn't do this **alone**. I asked my (older) sister to help me, and she has been a (great) **coach**. She is helping me to **raise** my (grades) in **most** of my subjects. She (won't) let me slip **away** to (play video games.) She (makes) me (stay) **awake** until I finish all my (homework.) She marks the (mistakes) in my work with a **crayon**.

Word Building
Verbs tell about actions. Many past-tense verbs end in –**ed**. Some verbs do not end with –**ed**. These are called **irregular verbs**. Look at each irregular past-tense verb in the box. Find the present tense of the verb in the numbered list. Then, write the past-tense verb next to the present tense verb.

took	hung	laid	made
froze	spoke	came	chose

1. speak   **spoke**
2. freeze   **froze**
3. make   **made**
4. lay   **laid**
5. choose   **chose**
6. hang   **hung**
7. take   **took**
8. come   **came**

15

Page 16

Fun with Words
Write the spelling word that completes each sign.

1. Do not swim in the pool **alone**
2. PLEASE Help Us Reach Our **goal** Of Selling 100 Boxes Of Cookies.
3. Stay **away** from the lions.
4. Come To The Soccer Field At 4:00 To Meet Our New **coach**
5. Vote NO to **raise** the price Of Soda.
6. Make the **most** of your library. Read a book every week!

Words Across the Curriculum
Say each social studies word. Then, write the word.

1. vote   **vote**
2. locate   **locate**
3. scale   **scale**
4. police   **police**

Write the social studies word that completes each sentence.

1. A map **scale** can tell how many miles one inch represents.
2. The duty of **police** officers is to protect people.
3. A map helps you **locate** different places.
4. Every citizen in this country has the right to **vote**.

16

Page 17

Words in Writing
Think about a goal that you would like to set for yourself. Write a paragraph that explains how you could meet this goal. Use at least four words from the box.

goal	away	alone	chose	coach	vote	scale
fail	most	awake	crayon	raise	locate	police

Answers will vary.

Misspelled Words
Read the paragraph. Circle the five misspelled words. Then, write the words correctly on the lines below.

My bedroom is usually a mess. Sometimes, there is a (trale) of clothes on the floor. I can't (locait) anything because (moste) of my things are scattered everywhere. So, I'm going to set a goal to clean my room every Saturday morning as soon as I'm (awaike.) During the week, I'll try to put things (awaye) when I'm finished using them.

trail	most	away
locate	awake	

17

Answer Key

Say each word. Listen for the long **e** or long **i** sound. Then, write the word.

Spelling Tips	The long **e** sound can be spelled **e, ee, ea, y,** or **ay**. The symbol for the long **e** sound is /ē/. The long **i** sound can be spelled **i-consonant-e, y,** or **igh**. The symbol for the long **i** sound is /ī/.

Spelling Words

high	high
easy	easy
wheel	wheel
busy	busy
smile	smile
street	street
lucky	lucky
wipe	wipe
might	might
between	between

18

Words in Context
Write the missing spelling words.

	Challenge
	Circle the other words in the article that have the /ē/ or /ī/ sound.

Our Class Car Wash

Last week, the students in my class had a car wash. We were afraid that it **might** rain, but we were **lucky**. By noon, the sun was **high** in the sky with no sign of any clouds. We set up our car wash **between** two buildings on the main **street** in town. A lot of people wanted their cars washed, so we were all very **busy**. It wasn't **easy** to scrub and **wipe** off the cars until they were clean and shiny. We even made sure that every **wheel** was free of dirt. Every one of our customers left with a **smile**.

Word Building
The ending **-y** is added to some nouns to make adjectives. Add **y** to each word to make an adjective. Then, write the adjective.
Example: **luck lucky**

1. rain **y**   rainy
2. moss **y**   mossy
3. dust **y**   dusty
4. rock **y**   rocky
5. wind **y**   windy
6. bump **y**   bumpy
7. pick **y**   picky
8. crust **y**   crusty

19

Fun with Words
Write the missing vowels that complete the spelling words.

1. sm **i** l **e**
2. str **e** **e** t
3. **e** **a** s **y**
4. w **i** p **e**
5. m **i** ght
6. luck **y**
7. h **i** gh
8. bus **y**
9. b **e** tw **e** **e** n
10. wh **e** **e** l

Words Across the Curriculum
Say each math word. Then, write the word.

1. mile   mile
2. twice   twice
3. area   area
4. equal   equal

Write the math words that complete the word problem.

Mike's ranch is shaped like a rectangle. It is one **mile** long on two sides, so these sides are **equal** to one another. The other two sides are **twice** as long as the first two. What is the **area** of Mike's ranch?

20

Words in Writing
Imagine your class needs to raise money for a class field trip. What ideas do you have about how to raise the money? Write the words for a poster advertising one of your ideas. Use at least four words from the box.

high	wheel	smile	lucky	might	mile	area
easy	busy	street	wipe	between	twice	equal

Answers will vary.

Dictionary Practice
Look at each pair of guide words. Circle the word that comes between the two words in alphabetical order.

1. easy—elf   end   edge   equal
2. smile—spot   square   staff   spoon
3. weep—wipe   won   want   wheel
4. boss—busy   break   by   blank
5. might—must   myth   more   math
6. bath—black   between   break   both

21

Answer Key

Say each word. Listen for the /ū/ sound. Then, write the word.

Spelling Tips	The /ū/ sound can be spelled ew, o-consonant-e, oo, ue, and u-consonant-e.

Spelling Words

cool	cool
rule	rule
lose	lose
noon	noon
true	true
move	move
mood	mood
grew	grew
clue	clue
scoop	scoop

22

Words in Context
Write the missing spelling words.

(Movie Review)

Challenge
Circle the other words in the article that have the /ū/ sound.

Yesterday, I went to see a (movie). It started at __noon__, and I was several minutes early. I had a __scoop__ of ice cream while I waited for (Sue). There was a (new) __rule__ at the theater that (food) isn't allowed inside. I ate my ice cream outside in the __cool__ weather. When (Sue) got there, we went inside to (choose) our seats.

The (movie) was a __true__ story about a family that was about to __lose__ their farm. The crops that they __grew__ had died because there hadn't been enough (rain). The family was going to have to __move__ out (soon). All their bills were (overdue). The __mood__ of the (movie) was mostly sad. But there was a __clue__ that the ending would turn out well.

Word Building
The story is **not true**. It is **untrue**.
The prefix **un-** means *not*. When un is added to the beginning of a word, the word means the opposite. Add **un** to each word. Then, write the word.

1. __un__ do   __undo__   4. __un__ lucky   __unlucky__
2. __un__ pack   __unpack__   5. __un__ safe   __unsafe__
3. __un__ like   __unlike__   6. __un__ dress   __undress__

23

Fun with Words
Write the spelling word that fits each meaning. Then, circle the letters to solve the riddle.

1. became bigger   (g)rew   Circle letter 1.
2. midday   r(oo)n   Circle letters 2 and 3.
3. unable to find something   lo(se)   Circle letters 3 and 4.
4. a law or order   ru(l)e   Circle letter 3.
5. a feeling   m(oo)d   Circle letters 2 and 3.
6. to lift up and out   (s)coop   Circle letter 1.
7. real   tru(e)   Circle letter 4.

What do you call a big bird that's running free?

A g o o s e on the l o o s e

Words Across the Curriculum
Say each science word. Then, write the word.

1. dew   __dew__   3. root   __root__
2. dune   __dune__   4. pollute   __pollute__

Write the science word next to its meaning.

1. a hill of sand   __dune__
2. water droplets   __dew__
3. a plant part   __root__
4. to spoil or make dirty   __pollute__

24

Words in Writing
Write a summary of a movie that you like. Use at least four words from the box.

cool	lose	true	mood	clue	dew	root
rule	noon	move	grew	scoop	pollute	dune

Answers will vary.

Misspelled Words
Read the summary. Circle the five misspelled words. Then, write the words correctly on the lines below.

I just saw the movie *You Can't Catch Me!* It was a mystery, but it was based on a (trew) story. It was about a detective who kept trying to catch a spy. The (mude) of the movie was exciting. Every time the detective found a new (clew), the suspense (grue). He would be close to finding the spy, but then he would (loose) track of her.

__true__	__clue__	__lose__
__mood__	__grew__	

25

Spectrum Spelling
Grade 3

Answer Key

157

Answer Key

Write the spelling word that means the same or nearly the same.

1. end   finish
2. simple   easy
3. many   lots
4. lift   raise
5. road   street
6. law   rule
7. garbage   trash
8. picked   chose

Write the spelling word that means the opposite.

1. pass   fail
2. winter   summer
3. midnight   noon
4. die   live
5. asleep   awake
6. false   true

26

Write the spelling word that belongs with each pair of words.

1. marker, chalk,   crayon
2. sport, activity,   hobby
3. face, neck,   head
4. teacher, tutor,   coach
5. grin, laugh,   smile
6. shovel, dig,   scoop

Write the spelling word that completes each sentence.

1. I fed some bread to a ___flock___ of birds. After they ate, the birds flew ___away___.
2. We climbed over a wooden ___fence___ to get to our campsite. Then, we set up our tent and closed the ___flap___.
3. Lin gave her baby brother a ___bath___ in the tub. Afterwards, she dried his ___damp___ skin with a soft towel.
4. I'm ___ready___ to go to my grandparents' house. I like to ___visit___ them.
5. Ari scored the winning ___goal___ in the soccer game. He kicked the ball ___high___ up into the top-left corner.
6. After I wandered along the river, I had to ___wipe___ the mud from my feet. Then, I walked on some soft, green ___moss___.

27

Say each word. Listen to the ending sound. Then, write the word.

Spelling Tips	The double consonants used most often at the ends of words include **ll**, **ff**, and **ss**.

Spelling Words

well	well
miss	miss
puff	puff
fill	fill
smell	smell
guess	guess
spill	spill
stuff	stuff
unless	unless
grill	grill

28

Words in Context
Write the missing spelling words.

Summer Cookout

Challenge
Circle the other words in the article that have double final consonants.

Our neighbor, Mr. Martin, always has a great cookout at the beginning of summer. It's so much fun that I would never ___miss___ it ___unless___ I were (ill.) Around two o'clock on Saturday, you can see a ___puff___ of smoke rising from the (small hill) in his yard. Then, everyone knows that Mr. Martin has started to cook.

Soon, the yard begins to ___fill___ up with people. Everyone tries to ___guess___ what type of food Mr. Martin (will) serve. There's always a wonderful ___smell___ coming from his ___grill___. You can't always (tell) what he's cooking. (Still,) he cooks so ___well___ that we (all) (now it) (will) be delicious. Mr. Martin doesn't mind if we ___spill___ our soda or make a (mess.) After we eat, some of us run (off) to do other fun ___stuff___, like play tag or (kickball.)

Word Building
The green ball is **small**. The blue ball is **smaller**. The red ball is the **smallest**. Add **er** and **est** to make new words that compare two or more things.

1. few   fewer   fewest
2. tall   taller   tallest
3. light   lighter   lightest

29

Answer Key

Page 30

Fun with Words

Write the spelling words that complete the puzzle.

Down
1. to pack tightly
2. to cook on open flames
3. odor

Across
2. an answer you're not sure of
4. in a good way or state
5. to make full

Crossword:
1. s
2. g u e s s
   t r m
   u i (4.) w e l l
5. f i l l   l
   f   l

Words Across the Curriculum

Say each science word. Then, write the word.

1. mass ___mass___   3. cliff ___cliff___
2. chill ___chill___   4. fall ___fall___

Write the science word next to its meaning.

1. to make cold ___chill___
2. the season after summer ___fall___
3. a steep rock formation ___cliff___
4. the amount of matter in an object ___mass___

Page 31

Words in Writing

Write a description of something you like to do in the summer. Use at least four words from the box.

| well | puff | smell | spill | unless | mass | cliff |
| miss | fill | guess | stuff | grill | chill | fall |

Answers will vary.

Dictionary Practice

Look at the dictionary entries. Then, answer the questions.

stuff /stuf/ **n. 1.** a collection of things. **2.** the material something is made of. **v. 1.** To cram or pack tightly.

well /wel/ **n. 1.** A hole in the ground that contains a supply of water. **2.** a shaft in the ground used to pump oil and gas. **adj. 1.** To be in good health. **2.** In a good way.

1. Which word can be used as a noun and an adjective? ___well___
2. As a verb, what does *stuff* mean? ___to cram or pack tightly___
3. How many definitions for the noun form of *well* are given? ___two___
4. Which word has the /e/ sound? ___well___

Page 32

Say each word. Listen to the ending sound. Then, write the word.

| Spelling Tips | The /el/ sound at the ends of words is often spelled **le**. |

Spelling Words

settle	___settle___
eagle	___eagle___
rattle	___rattle___
saddle	___saddle___
cattle	___cattle___
middle	___middle___
ripple	___ripple___
turtle	___turtle___
single	___single___
pebble	___pebble___

Page 33

Words in Context

Write the missing spelling words.

Challenge

Circle the other words in the story that have the final /el/ sound.

The West

There are still places in the West where hardly any pioneers decided to ___settle___. If you can (handle) a horse, you can put a ___saddle___ on him and ride out into the ___middle___ of nowhere. You might not see a ___single___ person all day. You might see an ___eagle___ soaring in the sky or a herd of ___cattle___ grazing on (little) patches of grass. You might even hear the ___rattle___ of a snake. You might also see a rushing river (tumble) over huge rocks much larger than a ___pebble___. Or, you might see a ___turtle___ poke its head out of a stream and make a small ___ripple___ in the water. All of these (simple) things make the West a (special) place.

Word Building

| tumble | candle | rattle | turtle |

Write the word from the box that can be added to each word below to make a compound word. Then, write the compound word.

1. ___rattle___ + snake = ___rattlesnake___
2. ___turtle___ + neck = ___turtleneck___
3. ___tumble___ + weed = ___tumbleweed___
4. ___candle___ + light = ___candlelight___

Answer Key

Fun with Words

Write the spelling word that completes each sentence and contains the word in **bold**.

1. The **cat** ran away from the herd of _____ cattle _____.
2. The children decided to _____ settle _____ down and play with a **set** of blocks.
3. I was **sad** when my horse's old _____ saddle _____ wore out.
4. The **rip** in the flag made it _____ ripple _____ in the wind.
5. That **rat** likes to _____ rattle _____ its cage.

Words Across the Curriculum

Say each social studies word. Then, write the word.

1. battle _____ battle _____   3. castle _____ castle _____
2. jungle _____ jungle _____   4. maple _____ maple _____

Write the social studies word that completes each sentence.

1. The old _____ castle _____ is protected by high, stone walls and a moat.
2. Parrots, monkeys, and snakes live in a tropical _____ jungle _____.
3. A _____ maple _____ leaf is the symbol on the flag of Canada.
4. The two armies met in a terrible _____ battle _____.

34

Words in Writing

Write a description of a place in nature that you like. Use at least four words from the box.

| settle | rattle | cattle | ripple | single | battle | jungle |
| eagle | saddle | middle | turtle | pebble | castle | maple |

Answers will vary.

Misspelled Words

Read the description. Circle the five misspelled words. Then, write the words correctly on the lines below.

I like to sit under the (maple) tree by the pond. Sometimes, I throw a (pebbele) into the (middel) of the water. The (singel) ripple it makes soon turns into many other little ripples. They sometimes disturb a (turtel) or a frog sitting near the edge of the pond. Soon, the water is calm again.

_____ maple _____   _____ middle _____   _____ turtle _____
_____ pebble _____   _____ single _____

35

Say each word. Listen to the middle consonant sound. Then, write the word.

| Spelling Tips | The middle consonant sounds in two-syllable words are sometimes spelled with double consonants. |

Spelling Words

letter	_____ letter _____
dollar	_____ dollar _____
happen	_____ happen _____
better	_____ better _____
rabbit	_____ rabbit _____
hammer	_____ hammer _____
soccer	_____ soccer _____
dinner	_____ dinner _____
zipper	_____ zipper _____
ladder	_____ ladder _____

36

Words in Context

Write the missing spelling words.

| Challenge |
| Circle the other two-syllable words in the story with double consonants in the middle. |

Shopping Trip

Last weekend, I went to the mall to shop. I dropped a _____ letter _____ in the mailbox for my mother on my way to the mall. When I got there, I walked around looking in the shop windows. I saw a nice jacket, but I didn't like the _____ zipper _____ on the front. I like (buttons) _____ better _____. I also saw some (funny slippers) that were each shaped like a _____ rabbit _____ with long, floppy ears. They were on sale for only a _____ dollar _____, so I bought them. I also bought some _____ soccer _____ cleats.

When I got to the last shop, I saw a man on a tall _____ ladder _____ using a _____ hammer _____ to nail a sign over the door. I was afraid that an (accident) would _____ happen _____ if I walked under him. So, I decided to go home. It was almost time to eat _____ dinner _____ anyway.

Word Building

Some nouns with one syllable and a short vowel sound double the last consonant when **er** and **est** are added to make adjectives. Double the last consonant in each word and add **er** and **est**.

1. wet _____ wetter _____   _____ wettest _____
2. sad _____ sadder _____   _____ saddest _____
3. hot _____ hotter _____   _____ hottest _____

37

Answer Key

Page 38

Fun with Words

Write the spelling word that fits each relationship.

1. **Steps** are to **staircase** as **rungs** are to ___ladder___.

2. **Tennis** is to **court** as ___soccer___ is to **field**.

3. **Worse** is to **bad** as ___better___ is to **best**.

4. **Kitty** is to **cat** as **bunny** is to ___rabbit___.

5. **Lace** is to **shoe** as ___zipper___ is to **coat**.

6. **Screwdriver** is to **screw** as ___hammer___ is to **nail**.

7. **Picture** is to **paint** as ___letter___ is to **write**.

8. **Lunch** is to **afternoon** as ___dinner___ is to **evening**.

Words Across the Curriculum

Say each science word. Then, write the word.

1. mammal ___mammal___   3. litter ___litter___

2. pulley ___pulley___   4. matter ___matter___

Write the science word that belongs with each pair of words.

1. wedge, lever, ___pulley___

2. mass, volume, ___matter___

3. reptile, bird, ___mammal___

4. trash, garbage ___litter___

38

Page 39

Words in Writing

Write a letter to a friend. Use at least four words from the box.

| letter | happen | rabbit | soccer | zipper | mammal | pulley |
| dollar | better | hammer | dinner | ladder | litter | matter |

Answers will vary.

Dictionary Practice

Circle the word in each pair that is correctly divided into syllables. Use the dictionary in the back if you need help.

1. dinner   di-nner   (din-ner)

2. accident   acc-id-ent   (ac-ci-dent)

3. possible   (pos-si-ble)   po-ssib-le

4. soccer   so-ccer   (soc-cer)

5. tomorrow   (to-mor-row)   tom-orr-ow

6. buffalo   buff-al-o   (buf-fa-lo)

39

Page 40

Say each word. Listen to the ending sound. Then, write the word.

| Spelling Tips | When a verb ends in **e**, the **e** is usually dropped before the –ed and –ing endings are added. |

Spelling Words

making	making
shining	shining
hiked	hiked
having	having
hoped	hoped
skated	skated
hiding	hiding
baked	baked
diving	diving
riding	riding

40

Page 41

Words in Context

Write the missing spelling words.

Challenge
Circle the other words in the journal entry whose final **e** was dropped before **ed** or **ing** was added.

Today was my first day at camp. I had ___hoped___ that I would really like it here, and I do. So far, I've been ___having___ a good time. When I woke up, I looked out the window and saw that the sun was ___shining___. While I was ___making___ my bed, two boys stopped by my cabin and (invited) me to go horseback ___riding___ with them. First, we walked over to the main building and ate freshly ___baked___ muffins and eggs for breakfast. Then, we ___hiked___ up a hill to the barn. We rode horses around the whole camp. We saw some campers ___diving___ into the lake and (chasing) each other along the shore. A few other campers ___skated___ along the path by the lake. I thought I saw some deer ___hiding___ in the woods.

Word Building

Write the base word next to each spelling word. Then, add the other ending to the word.

1. hiked ___hike___   ___hiking___

2. skated ___skate___   ___skating___

3. baked ___bake___   ___baking___

4. shined ___shine___   ___shining___

41

Answer Key

Fun with Words

Write the spelling word that completes each tongue-twister.

1. My mom is ___making___ many more muffins.
2. Henry ___hoped___ his horse hadn't hurt her hoof.
3. Six ships sailed south under the ___shining___ summer sun.
4. Ben ___baked___ bread before beginning to broil the beef.
5. Skip sledded, skied, and ___skated___ on some slippery surfaces.
6. Dan discovered a dozen ___diving___ dolphins.
7. Hundreds of hens were ___hiding___ from hungry hunters.
8. Harry is ___having___ his helper hold his hat.

Words Across the Curriculum

Say each art word. Then, write the word.

1. creating ___creating___   3. shaping ___shaping___
2. glazed ___glazed___   4. fired ___fired___

Write the missing art words.

I like ___creating___ things with clay. I begin by ___shaping___ the clay into a form. Then, I put it into a kiln, where the clay form is ___fired___. Sometimes, I coat the form with clear paint. This gives the form a ___glazed___ look.

42

Words in Writing

Write an invitation to a party you would like to have. Use at least four words from the box.

| making | hiked | hoped | hiding | diving | creating | shaping |
| shining | having | skated | baked | riding | glazed | fired |

Answers will vary.

Misspelled Words

Read the invitation. Circle the five misspelled words. Then, write the words correctly on the lines below.

I am (haveing) a pool party next Saturday. I hope the sun is (shineing) so we can all go swimming and (diveing) in the pool. Then, I will be (makeing) hamburgers for dinner. We'll also have (bakede) potatoes. I hope you can come!

___having___   ___diving___   ___baked___
___shining___   ___making___

43

Write the spelling words that mean the same or almost the same.

1. hare ___rabbit___
2. creating ___making___
3. odor ___smell___
4. stone ___pebble___
5. supper ___dinner___
6. note ___letter___

Write the spelling word that belongs with each pair of words.

1. broil, bake, ___grill___
2. frog, snail, ___turtle___
3. walked, climbed, ___hiked___
4. button, hook, ___zipper___
5. pack, cram, ___stuff___
6. alone, one, ___single___
7. bright, gleaming, ___shining___
8. good, best, ___better___

44

Write the spelling word that rhymes with each pair of words.

1. mess, less, ___guess___
2. raked, faked, ___baked___
3. tell, sell, ___well___
4. locker, rocker, ___soccer___
5. rated, waited, ___skated___
6. kiss, hiss, ___miss___

Write the spelling word that completes each sentence.

1. A ___puff___ of smoke rose from the fire.
2. Please use the ___hammer___ to pound the nail.
3. I ___hoped___ that I got a good grade on my test.
4. A duck was swimming in the ___middle___ of the pond.
5. Each balloon costs one ___dollar___.
6. My dad climbed the ___ladder___ to fix the roof.
7. The ___eagle___ made a nest on a high cliff.
8. I put the ___saddle___ on my horse and went for a ride.

45

Answer Key

Say each word. Listen for the /oi/ sound. Then, write the word.

Spelling Tips	The /oi/ sound can be spelled **oi** and **oy**.

Spelling Words

point	point
noise	noise
voice	voice
enjoy	enjoy
join	join
loyal	loyal
annoy	annoy
choice	choice
spoil	spoil
avoid	avoid

46

Words in Context
Write the missing spelling words.

Challenge
Circle the other words in the story with the /oi/ sound.

Soccer Is a Team Sport

I recently decided to ___join___ a (boys') soccer team. I really ___enjoy___ playing on the team. We are all very ___loyal___ to one another. We ___avoid___ any kind of trouble that might ___spoil___ our (joy) of playing the game. If we have a ___choice___ to pass the ball or shoot it, we do whatever will help the team make a goal and score a ___point___.
    We try not to listen to people on the sidelines who shout in an angry ___voice___ and make a lot of ___noise___. Sometimes, they really ___annoy___ us, but we don't them (destroy) our fun.

Word Building
Add the ending **-ing** to each word below.

1. enjoy ___enjoying___
2. point ___pointing___
3. join ___joining___
4. avoid ___avoiding___
5. spoil ___spoiling___
6. annoy ___annoying___
7. broil ___broiling___
8. destroy ___destroying___

47

Fun with Words
Write the vowels to complete spelling word.

1. l_o_y_a_l
2. v_o_i_c_e
3. n_o_i_s_e
4. _a_nn_o_y
5. _a_v_o_i_d
6. p_o_i_nt
7. ch_o_i_c_e
8. _e_nj_o_y

Words Across the Curriculum
Say each science word. Then, write the word.

1. soil ___soil___
2. oyster ___oyster___
3. boiling ___boiling___
4. poison ___poison___

Write the science word next to its meaning.

1. an ocean animal that lives in a shell ___oyster___
2. the state of a liquid when it is very hot ___boiling___
3. a layer of earth made of small particles ___soil___
4. a substance that is harmful to animals or plants ___poison___

48

Words in Writing
Write a newspaper article about a sports event you saw. Use at least four words from the box.

point	voice	join	annoy	spoil	soil	boiling
noise	enjoy	loyal	choice	avoid	oyster	poison

Answers will vary.

Dictionary Practice
Decide which words in the box belong in each column below. Then, write the words in each column in alphabetical order.

Words with One Syllable	Words with Two Syllables
boil	annoy
choice	avoid
join	enjoy
noise	loyal
point	oyster
soil	poison
spoil	voice

49

Answer Key

Say each word. Listen for the /ou/ sound. Then, write the word.

Spelling Tips	The /ou/ sound can be spelled **ou** and **ow**.

Spelling Words

about	about
frown	frown
tower	tower
cloud	cloud
flower	flower
mouth	mouth
allow	allow
shout	shout
amount	amount
shower	shower

50

Words in Context
Write the missing spelling words.

Challenge
Circle the other words in the story with the /ou/ sound.

Money Isn't Everything

Once, there was a king who liked to shut himself up in the _____ **tower** of his castle. He locked the door and didn't _____ **allow** anyone to enter. The king spent many (hours) every day (counting) his money, but the _____ **amount** was never enough for him. Every time he finished (counting) his money, the corners of his _____ **mouth** drooped (down) into a _____ **frown**.

One day, the king heard a (loud sound) coming from (outside) his window. He looked (outside) and saw a heavy _____ **shower** of rain falling to the (ground). He heard someone _____ **shout** his name, but he couldn't see anyone there. The king hurried (down) into his _____ **flower** garden. He looked (around) but saw no one. Even more surprising to the king, it wasn't raining in his garden. There wasn't a single _____ **cloud** in the sky. The king sat down to think _____ **about** this. He saw for the first time that his garden was beautiful. He decided that he had let the (power) of money rule him. From (now) on, he would try to enjoy other things.

Word Building
Add the word **ground** or **out** to each word below to form a compound word.

1. back **background**
2. cook **cookout**
3. look **lookout**
4. play **playground**

51

Fun with Words
Write the spelling word that completes each sentence and rhymes with the word in **bold**.

1. You can **count** an _____ **amount** of money.
2. When the king lost his **crown**, he started to _____ **frown** .
3. The thunder from the _____ **cloud** was very **loud**.
4. The farmer will _____ **allow** the **cow** to go out.
5. The light spring _____ **shower** fell gently on the **flower**.
6. The children ran **out** of school with a _____ **shout** .
7. The **scout** told us _____ **about** the camp.
8. The **power** of the wind knocked down the _____ **tower** .

Words Across the Curriculum
Say each math word. Then, write the word.

1. ounce **ounce**
2. thousand **thousand**
3. round **round**
4. pound **pound**

Write the math word that completes each sentence.

1. The smallest unit of weight in the English system is an _____ **ounce** .
   Sixteen of these units equal one _____ **pound** .
2. When you don't need an exact answer, you can _____ **round** a number to the nearest, ten, hundred, or _____ **thousand** .

52

Words in Writing
Write a poem about nature. Use at least four words from the box.

| about | tower | flower | allow | amount | ounce | round |
| frown | cloud | mouth | shout | shower | thousand | pound |

Answers will vary.

Misspelled Words
Read the poem. Circle the four misspelled words. Then, write the words correctly on the lines below.

Winter is (abowt) to end,
And spring is almost here.
(Clowds) will bring gentle (shouers)
To water (thosands) of flowers.

about	showers
clouds	thousands

53

Answer Key

Say each word. Listen for the /ô/ sound. Then, write the word.

Spelling Tips	The /ô/ sound can be spelled **a, aw,** or **o**.

Spelling Words

because	because
talk	talk
lawn	lawn
frost	frost
dawn	dawn
paw	paw
thaw	thaw
caught	caught
across	across
stalk	stalk

54

Words in Context
Write the missing spelling words.

Challenge
Circle the other words in the description that have the /ô/ sound.

A Winter Morning

This morning, I got up at ___dawn___. My older brother Josh was already awake. We decided to go for a (walk) in the woods. Josh and I put on heavy coats and boots ___because___ it was very cold outside. We (walked) ___across___ our front ___lawn___. Every blade of grass and dried-out flower ___stalk___ was covered with ___frost___. It wouldn't start to ___thaw___ out until later in the day.

When we got to the woods, Josh and I stayed quiet and didn't ___talk___ to each other. We (saw) some ___paw___ prints in the snow. We looked up and ___caught___ sight of some deer and a much (smaller) spotted (fawn). The deer (paused) for a minute, and then they disappeared into the woods.

Word Building
Add the **–ed** ending to each word below to make the past-tense verb. Then, write the new verb.

1. frost _ed_	frosted		4. crawl _ed_	crawled
2. talk _ed_	talked		5. walk _ed_	walked
3. thaw _ed_	thawed		6. haunt _ed_	haunted

55

Fun with Words
Write the spelling word that answers each riddle.

1. I am cold and white. I arrive overnight. What am I? ___frost___

2. I am green and neat. I feel good under bare feet. What am I? ___lawn___

3. I begin the days. I have soft, glowing rays. What am I? ___dawn___

4. I am attached to a flower. I can be straight and strong as a tower. What am I? ___stalk___

5. I am like a hand or foot. I sometimes make a print, but not on paper. What am I? ___paw___

6. I am an action. I heat cold things. What am I? ___thaw___

Words Across the Curriculum
Say each art word. Then, write the word.

1. draw	draw	3. chalk	chalk
2. straw	straw	4. gloss	gloss

Write the art word that completes each analogy.

1. **Pot** is to **clay** as **basket** is to ___straw___.
2. **Paint** is to **brush** as ___draw___ is to **pencil**.
3. **Dull** is to **matte** as shiny is to ___gloss___.
4. **Drops** is to **paint** as **dust** is to ___chalk___.

56

Words in Writing
Write a description of a winter day.
Use at least four words from the box.

because	lawn	dawn	thaw	across	draw	chalk
talk	frost	paw	caught	stalk	straw	gloss

Answers will vary.

Dictionary Practice
Read the dictionary entries. Then, read the sentences below. Write **noun** or **verb** to tell what part of speech each word in bold is.

saw /sô/ **n. 1.** A metal tool with teethlike points used for cutting. **v. 1.** To cut with a saw. **2.** The past tense of *see*.

stalk /stôk/ **n. 1.** The main stem of a plant. **2.** A supporting part: the stalk of a lobster's eye. **v. 1.** To hunt or track quietly. **2.** To walk in a stiff, determined way.

1. The lion **stalked** its prey. ___verb___
2. I **saw** the sun rise in the morning. ___verb___
3. The teeth of the **saw** cut into the wood. ___noun___
4. The tulip's **stalk** is tall and straight. ___noun___

57

Spectrum Spelling
Grade 3

Answer Key

Answer Key

Page 62

Fun with Words

Write the spelling words that complete each sentence. The spelling words in each sentence will be homophones of each other.

1. **Would** you like to buy some **wood** ?
2. I can **not** untie this **knot** .
3. Make sure that you **write** the **right** spelling words.
4. I am at **peace** in this little **piece** of the park.
5. Sue will **sew** the rip in her dress **so** she can wear it tonight.

Words Across the Curriculum

Say each pair of words that sound the same. Look at the different spellings. Then, write the words.

1. cent **cent**
2. sent **sent**
3. whole **whole**
4. hole **hole**
5. greater **greater**
6. grater **grater**
7. pair **pair**
8. pear **pear**

Write the math homophone from each pair above that completes each sentence.

1. The number 27 is **greater** than the number 24.
2. The value of a penny is one **cent** .
3. All the fractional parts of an object equal the **whole** object.
4. A number **pair** can be plotted as a point on a grid.

62

Page 63

Words in Writing

Write a list of things you would do to set up a campsite. Use at least four words from the box.

so	not	wood	write	piece	cent	greater	pair	whole
sew	knot	would	right	peace	sent	grater	pear	hole

Answers will vary.

Misspelled Words

Read the list of things to do. Circle the five misspelled words. Then, write the words correctly on the lines below.

Make sure the tent is set up (rite).
Chop some pieces of (woud) (soo) we can make a fire.
(Wright) a list of camp rules.
Enjoy the (paece) and quiet of nature.

right   **so**   **peace**
wood   **Write**

63

Page 64

Look at each word. Say the word. Then, write the word.

Spelling Tips	A **contraction** is made of two words with one or more letters left out. An **apostrophe** is a mark that shows that some letters have been left out.

Spelling Words

I'd	**I'd**
he'd	**he'd**
she'll	**she'll**
you're	**you're**
I've	**I've**
they'll	**they'll**
weren't	**weren't**
we've	**we've**
you'll	**you'll**
wouldn't	**wouldn't**

64

Page 65

Words in Context

Write the missing spelling words.

Picnic Invitation

Challenge
Circle the other contractions in the invitation.

Dear Ben,

(I'm) writing to let you know that **you're** invited to a picnic next Saturday. **I'd** really like you come. (We're) all going to meet at Riverside Park at two o'clock. Mia and Jon are helping me plan the picnic. **They'll** bring the food and drinks. Mia said that **she'll** make sandwiches and salad. Jon said that **he'd** bring soda and ice. (He's) also going to bring some cookies. **I've** decided to bring my soccer ball, but my mom said she **wouldn't** let me bring my hockey sticks. She (doesn't) think (it's) a good idea.

I think that Mia, Jon, and I have planned the picnic pretty well. **We've** invited about thirty other people. At first, we **weren't** going to invite so many people. Then, we decided that (we'd) have more fun with a big group. I hope you can join us! I'm sure **you'll** have a great time.

Your friend,
Tony

65

Answer Key

Fun with Words

Circle the two words in each question that form a contraction that is a spelling word. Switch the order of the words. Then, write the contraction on the line after the sentence.

1. (Have we) got time for a snack? — we've
2. (Will she) come to our party? — she'll
3. (Will you) have tea with me? — you'll
4. (Are you) ready to go? — you're
5. (Have I) passed the test? — I've
6. (Will they) come over to play? — they'll
7. (Would he) like to see my puppy? — he'd
8. (Would I) be able to go fishing at the lake? — I'd

Words Across the Curriculum

Say each contraction. Then, write the contraction.

1. it'll _____ it'll _____
2. shouldn't _____ shouldn't _____
3. you'd _____ you'd _____
4. they'd _____ they'd _____

Write the contraction that completes each sentence.

1. I think that _____ you'd _____ really enjoy reading this book.
2. The children said that _____ they'd _____ like to go swimming.
3. Do you think that _____ it'll _____ be a rainy day tomorrow?
4. You _____ shouldn't _____ go outside without a coat.

66

Words in Writing

Write an invitation asking a friend to come to a picnic or party. Use at least four words from the box.

I'd	she'll	I've	weren't	you'll	shouldn't	you'd
he'd	you're	they'll	we've	wouldn't	it'll	they'd

Answers will vary.

Dictionary Practice

Write the symbol for the vowel sound next to each word below.

/ā/	/ĭ/
/ē/	/ü/

1. I've _____ /ĭ/ _____   5. wouldn't _____ /ü/ _____
2. they'll _____ /ā/ _____   6. we've _____ /ē/ _____
3. he'd _____ /ē/ _____   7. they'd _____ /ā/ _____
4. I've _____ /ĭ/ _____   8. shouldn't _____ /ü/ _____

67

Look at each word. Say the word. Then, write the word.

> **Spelling Tips**
> Some words aren't spelled the way they sound. You have to remember how to spell them.

Spelling Words

done	done
other	other
always	always
never	never
school	school
learn	learn
favorite	favorite
again	again
work	work
picture	picture

68

Words in Context

Write the missing spelling words.

I Like Art

I like to _____ learn _____ about all kinds of things in _____ school _____. Still, art is my _____ favorite _____ subject. We _____ never _____ have to take a quiz or test in art class. Instead, we just _____ work _____ on our art projects. We don't _____ always _____ draw or paint a _____ picture _____. We also make _____ other _____ kinds of artwork. We make shapes with clay, and weave yarn to make cloth. After we have _____ done _____ a lot of different kinds of projects, we go back to painting _____ again _____.

Word Building

The prefix **un–** means **not** or **opposite**. Add the prefix **un–** to each word below to make a new word that means the opposite. Then, write the word.

1. un done — undone   5. un fold — unfold
2. un lock — unlock   6. un made — unmade
3. un button — unbutton   7. un load — unload
4. un even — uneven   8. un sure — unsure

69

Answer Key

Page 70

Fun with Words
Use the letters in each wo[...]rds.

Answers will vary.

1. other _____ or, the, rot, hot, to, toe, her, he
2. done _____ on, one, do, doe, nod, end, den, no
3. picture _____ it, rip, ripe, pit, tip, pure
4. favorite _____ it, or, rot, to, toe, fit, tore, for, at, fat
5. always _____ way, ways, as, was, saw, sway
6. learn _____ ear, an, near, real, lean

Words Across the Curriculum
Say each math word. Then, write the word.

1. square _____ square
2. triangle _____ triangle
3. circle _____ circle
4. sphere _____ sphere

Write the math word that completes each sentence.

1. A _____ triangle _____ has three straight sides.
2. The planet Earth is shaped like a _____ sphere _____ .
3. A _____ square _____ has four sides of equal length and four right angles.
4. A _____ circle _____ is a single curved line.

70

Page 71

Words in Writing
Write a description of a work of art that you like.
Use at least four words from the box.

| done | always | school | favorite | work | square | circle |
| other | never | learn | again | picture | triangle | sphere |

Answers will vary.

Misspelled Words
Read the description. Circle the five misspelled words. Then, write the words correctly on the lines below.

One of my favorete paintings is named *Rainy Night Downtown*. It's a picsure of a busy street. Squares, sircles, and other shapes represent buildings and signs. These shapes are repeated over and over agan. The colors in the painting are mostly light oranges and yellows. I've neaver seen any other painting like this one.

_____ favorite _____ circles _____ never
_____ picture _____ again

71

Page 72

Write the contraction for each pair of words.

1. she will _____ she'll
2. I have _____ I've
3. we have _____ we've
4. they will _____ they'll
5. I would _____ I'd
6. he would _____ he'd
7. were not _____ weren't
8. you are _____ you're
9. would not _____ wouldn't
10. you will _____ you'll

Write the spelling word that goes with each group of words.

1. part, segment, portion, _____ piece
2. correct, true, exact, _____ right
3. twigs, timber, lumber, _____ wood
4. stitch, seam, mend, _____ sew

72

Page 73

Write the spelling word that means the same or almost the same.

1. trapped _____ caught
2. finished _____ done
3. print _____ write
4. most liked _____ favorite
5. not ever _____ never
6. harmony _____ peace

Write the spelling word that completes each sentence.

1. Do you ride your bike to _____ school _____ every day?
2. I like to _____ learn _____ new things about the planets.
3. After the boys finished the game, they played it _____ again _____ .
4. Rob missed the bus, _____ so _____ he had to walk home.
5. Can you please untie this _____ knot _____ ?
6. There is a _____ picture _____ of my dad on the wall.
7. My dog _____ would _____ like to go for a walk.
8. On the weekends, a lot of people _____ work _____ in their yards.

73

Answer Key

Say each word. Listen to the beginning sound. Then, write the word.

Spelling Tips	The consonant blends **spl**, **spr**, and **str** are spelled the way they sound.

Spelling Words

splash	splash
strip	strip
strong	strong
spray	spray
stream	stream
spring	spring
split	split
sprout	sprout
spread	spread
strange	strange

74

Words in Context
Write the missing spelling words.

Challenge
Circle the other words in the description that begin with **spl**, **spr**, or **str**.

Alaska

Have you ever been to Alaska in the _____ spring _____? Some of the land is still (sprinkled) with snow, but a few plants are beginning to _____ sprout _____. Here and there, you might still see a _____ strip _____ of frozen ground.

Alaska has many rivers. One way to see this _____ strange _____ but beautiful land is to take a boat trip on a _____ stream _____. (Straight) ahead of you, the water seems to _____ split _____ the land in two. On each side, you can see the tundra _____ spread _____ out for miles and miles. You might see a salmon or other _____ strong _____ fish leap out of the water and _____ splash _____ back into it a few seconds later. These fish are so big that water drops might _____ spray _____ you even if you are far away. You can see many other (splendid) sights in Alaska.

Word Building
Add the ending **-ing** to each word. Then, write the new word.

1. sprout **ing**   sprouting
2. spread **ing**   spreading
3. spray **ing**   spraying
4. splash **ing**   splashing

75

Fun with Words
Use the letters in each spe[lling word to make] more smaller words with at least three le[tters.]

Answers will vary.

1. spring _____ ring, sip, pin, spin, nip, pig, sing
2. stream _____ meat, mate, team, seam, mast, eat, seat
3. spread _____ read, red, dare, dear, spear, pad, rap, sad
4. split _____ lit, spit, sit, sip, pit, lips, slit
5. spray _____ pay, ray, pray, say, rap, pry
6. strange _____ range, sang, sag, tan, tag, gear, tear, stag, sea, seat
7. strip _____ rip, trip, pit, sit, stir, sip
8. sprout _____ out, pot, rot, spot, stop, top, put, tour

Words Across the Curriculum
Say each art word. Then, write the word.

1. stripe _____ stripe   3. strum _____ strum
2. sprinkle _____ sprinkle   4. straight _____ straight

Write the art word that completes each sentence.

1. We listened to my father _____ strum _____ his guitar.
2. My favorite sweater has a white _____ stripe _____ down the middle.
3. You can draw a _____ straight _____ line with a ruler.
4. I decided to _____ sprinkle _____ some glitter on my painting.

76

Words in Writing
Write a description of a place you have visited. Use at least four words from the box.

splash	strong	stream	split	spread	stripe	strum
strip	spray	spring	sprout	strange	sprinkle	straight

_____

Answers will vary.

Dictionary Practice
Read the dictionary entries and sentences. Write **noun** or **verb** to tell what part of speech the word in bold is. Then, write the number of the definition.

spring /spring/ **n. 1.** The season after winter. **2.** A spiral-shaped piece of metal that returns to its shape after being stretched. **v. 1.** To move forward or jump up quickly. **2.** To grow suddenly or quickly.

spread /spred/ **n. 1.** A cloth covering for a bed. **2.** Soft food that can be used to cover bread or other solid food. **v. 1.** To unfold or stretch out. **2.** To cover with a thin layer of something.

1. The farmer **spread** seeds over the damp soil.   verb, 2
2. A broken **spring** stuck out of the mattress.   noun, 2
3. I like cheese **spread** on my crackers.   noun, 2
4. My brother likes to **spring** out from behind a door to scare me.   verb, 1

77

Answer Key

Say each word. Listen for the /s/ sound one or two times in the word. Then, write the word.

Spelling Tip	The /s/ sound can be spelled **s** or **c**. Some words have both spellings for the /s/ sound.

Spelling Words

rice	rice
silence	silence
sauce	sauce
place	place
spice	spice
center	center
juice	juice
erase	erase
pencil	pencil
since	since

78

Words in Context

My Favorite Restaurant

My favorite ___place___ to eat lunch is a small restaurant in the ___center___ of the city. Ever ___since___ my older sister first took me there, I've really liked it. The food is simple but very good. I usually get a bowl of ___rice___ and vegetables covered with a sweet ___sauce___. The cook adds exactly the amount of ___spice___ I like in my food.

The restaurant has a quiet patio in the back. My sister and I enjoy the ___silence___ of the patio and drink ___juice___ before we eat. Then, our server writes down our lunch order with a pad and ___pencil___. When we change our minds, he has to ___erase___ the order and write it again.

Challenge

Circle the other words in the description with the /s/ sound.

SPECIALS
YUMMY SOUP AND SPICED RICE

Word Building

You can add the ending –y to some nouns to make adjectives. When a noun ends in **e**, you usually drop the **e** before adding **y**. Drop the **e** and add **y** to each noun to make an adjective.
Example: **juice, juicy**

1. spice	spicy	4. shine	shiny
2. noise	noisy	5. taste	tasty
3. ice	icy	6. smoke	smoky

79

Fun with Words

Write the letters **s** and **c** to complete the spelling words.

1. **S** pi **C** e
2. pen **C** il
3. **S** au **C** e
4. ri **C** e
5. pla **C** e
6. era **S** e
7. **C** enter
8. **S** ilen **C** e
9. jui **C** e
10. **S** in **C** e

Words Across the Curriculum

Say each science word. Then, write the word.

1. cell — cell
2. sense — sense
3. cycle — cycle
4. science — science

Write the science words that complete each sentence.

1. ___Science___ is the study of the world around us.
2. A ___cell___ is the smallest part of a living thing that performs life functions.
3. You can use your ___sense___ of sight to observe things.
4. Water moves from oceans to clouds and back to Earth in an ongoing ___cycle___.

80

Words in Writing

Write a description of a meal that you like. Use at least four words from the box.

rice	sauce	spice	juice	pencil	cell	cycle
silence	place	center	erase	since	sense	science

Answers will vary.

Misspelled Words

Read the description. Circle the five misspelled words. Then, write the words correctly on the lines below.

One meal that I really like is chili with a lot of spise. I like to put a spoonful of chili in the senter of a bowl of risce. Then, I mix them together. I also like to have chips with my chili. I dip the chips in a cheese sause. Sometimes, I have tomato juise with my meal.

spice	rice	juice
center	sauce	

81

Answer Key

Say each word. Listen for the /j/ sound. Then, write the word.

Spelling Tip	The /j/ sound can be spelled **j**, **g**, or **ge**.

Spelling Words

joke	joke
gym	gym
large	large
page	page
stage	stage
giant	giant
range	range
magic	magic
jacket	jacket
judge	judge

82

Words in Context.
Write the missing spelling words.

Talent Show

> **Challenge**
> Circle the other words in the description that have the /j/ sound.

Our class is planning a talent show. We need a very ____large____ room to fit everyone who wants to come. So, we decided to use the school ____gym____ for the show. We've just set up the ____stage____ for the performers. We hung a ____giant____ curtain in front of it. We also made booklets with the names of all the performers on the first ____page____.

I'm going to be the host of the show. I'll wear a black ____jacket____ and a tie. I might tell a ____joke____ or two to make everyone feel less nervous. My friend Gina is going to do ____magic____ tricks. Jim will sing songs that show the ____range____ of his voice. We hope everyone will enjoy the show. Afterward, the audience will ____judge____ each performer.

Word Building
The ending **-er** often means someone or something that does something. When you add **er** to a verb that ends in **e**, drop the final **e** before adding **er**. Add **er** to each verb to make a noun.

1. joke	joker	4. race	racer
2. erase	eraser	5. write	writer
3. hike	hiker	6. move	mover

83

Fun with Words
Use the clues to complete the puzzle.

Across
1. decide
3. a trick or riddle
5. a large, open area used to put on a play

Down
1. a light coat
2. a place to exercise
4. huge

(crossword puzzle with answers: judge, jacket, gym, joke, stage, giant)

Words Across the Curriculum
Say each social studies word. Then, write the word.

1. general	general	3. wage	wage
2. journey	journey	4. religion	religion

Write each social studies word with the pair of words it belongs with.

1. job, pay,	wage
2. faith, belief,	religion
3. trip, travel,	journey
4. leader, army,	general

84

Words in Writing
What kind of act would you like to perform in a talent show? Write a description of the act that you would perform. Use at least four words from the box.

joke	large	stage	range	jacket	general	wage
gym	page	giant	magic	judge	journey	religion

Answers will vary.

Dictionary Practice
Write the words from the box in alphabetical order. For some words, you will have to look at the second or third letter.

1. general		8. large
2. giant		9. magic
3. gym		10. page
4. jacket		11. range
5. joke		12. religion
6. journey		13. stage
7. judge		14. wage

85

Answer Key

Say each word. Listen to the ending sound. Then, write the word.

Spelling Tip	For many nouns that end in **y**, drop the **y** and add **ies** to make the words mean more than one.

Spelling Words

penny	penny
pennies	pennies
lady	lady
ladies	ladies
puppy	puppy
puppies	puppies
city	city
cities	cities
party	party
parties	parties

86

Words in Context
Write the missing spelling words.

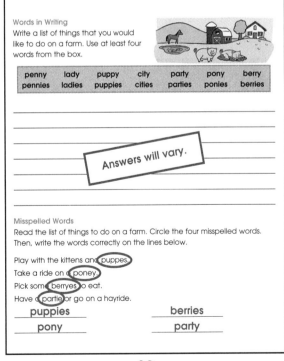

My Aunt Alice

In the summer, I leave the ____city____ for a week and go to the country. I visit my Aunt Alice there. She's a very nice ____lady____ who lives by herself on a farm.

Aunt Alice loves to have ____parties____. Last summer, her dog had four ____puppies____. Aunt Alice invited some other ____ladies____ to come over for a ____party____ to celebrate. Two of her friends traveled to Aunt Alice's farm from other ____cities____. She had promised to give each one of them a ____puppy____ to take home with them.

At the party, the children hunted for ____pennies____ that Aunt Alice had hidden in the grass. For every ____penny____ that we found, Aunt Alice changed it for a quarter.

Word Building
The words in the box are names of baby animals. Write the name of each baby animal next to the name of its parent.

| calf | kid | fawn | piglet |
| chick | duckling | kitten | puppy |

1. dog ____puppy____   5. duck ____duckling____
2. goat ____kid____   6. cat ____kitten____
3. deer ____fawn____   7. bird ____chick____
4. cow ____calf____   8. pig ____piglet____

87

Fun with Words
Write the spelling word that completes each poster.

1. Balloons For Sale Just one **penny** each.
2. Rent a peaceful cabin far away from the **city**
3. Good homes wanted for two-month old **puppies**
4. Garden Party 3 o'clock today at the **ladies** Club.
5. Visit New York one of the most exciting **cities** in the world.
6. Have you seen this lost **puppy**? Reward Of $25

Words Across the Curriculum
Say each science word. Then, write the word.

1. pony ____pony____   3. berry ____berry____
2. ponies ____ponies____   4. berries ____berries____

Write the missing science words.

1. Many children who live on farms ride ____ponies____. A ____pony____ looks like a horse, but it is much smaller.
2. A ____berry____ is a small fruit. There are many different kinds of ____berries____.

88

Words in Writing
Write a list of things that you would like to do on a farm. Use at least four words from the box.

| penny | lady | puppy | city | party | pony | berry |
| pennies | ladies | puppies | cities | parties | ponies | berries |

Answers will vary.

Misspelled Words
Read the list of things to do on a farm. Circle the four misspelled words. Then, write the words correctly on the lines below.

Play with the kittens and (puppes).
Take a ride on a (poney).
Pick some (berryes) to eat.
Have a (partie) or go on a hayride.

____puppies____   ____berries____
____pony____   ____party____

89

Answer Key

Write the spelling word that means the same or almost the same.

1. woman — **lady**
2. coat — **jacket**
3. odd — **strange**
4. middle — **center**
5. cent — **penny**
6. riddle — **joke**
7. river — **stream**
8. decide — **judge**

Write the spelling word that rhymes with each word.

1. flash — **splash**
2. loose — **juice**
3. change — **range**
4. guppy — **puppy**
5. long — **strong**
6. trout — **sprout**
7. him — **gym**
8. tray — **spray**

90

Write the spelling word that belongs with each pair of words.

1. divide, separate — **split**
2. person, thing — **place**
3. theater, play — **stage**
4. towns, villages — **cities**
5. summer, fall — **spring**
6. pen, marker — **pencil**

Write the spelling words that complete the description.

My family's house is in the middle of the **city**, but we have a very **large** backyard. On one side, there is a long **strip** of soil that we made into a flowerbed. In the spring, many flowers **sprout** there. Sometimes, we have **parties** in our yard for our friends. We also let our dog and her **puppies** run around in the yard.

91

Say each word. Listen for vowel and consonant sounds that you know. Then, write the word. Make sure that you use a capital letter to begin each day of the week.

Spelling Tip
Many words that name the days of the week and words that tell about time are spelled the way they sound. Others have unusual spellings. You have to remember how to spell these.

Spelling Words

Friday	**Friday**
Sunday	**Sunday**
morning	**morning**
Tuesday	**Tuesday**
Saturday	**Saturday**
evening	**evening**
Monday	**Monday**
afternoon	**afternoon**
Thursday	**Thursday**
Wednesday	**Wednesday**

92

Words in Context
Write the missing spelling words.

Challenge
Circle the other time words in the schedule.

A Busy Week

Now that the weekend is over, I have a very busy week ahead of me. On **Monday**, I have to go back to school in the **morning**. Then, I have soccer practice after school. On the next day, which is **Tuesday**, I have a piano lesson after school. There's another soccer practice the following day, on **Wednesday**.

On **Thursday**, I have to go home right after school to study for my math test. After school on **Friday**, I'm going to visit my grandmother. I'll have dinner with her and go home later in the **evening**.

The next day is **Saturday**, the first day of the weekend. When I get up, I have to do some chores. After lunch, I can do whatever I want for the rest of the **afternoon**. At 7:00 that evening, our team has a soccer match. Two of my teammates are going to stay overnight at my house. Then, on **Sunday**, all the people in my family are coming to my house for dinner. I have to help my mother get ready.

93

Spectrum Spelling
Grade 3

Answer Key

174

Answer Key

Answer Key

Fun with Words

Write the spelling word that fits each clue. The words in bold will help you.

1. You might have **fried** fish on this day. __Friday__

2. You might count your **money** on this day to make sure you have enough to last all week. __Monday__

3. If the **sun** is shining, this might be a good day to be outside. __Sunday__

4. This is day number **two** in the school week. __Tuesday__

5. There is much **more** time in a day after this time. __morning__

6. If you **sat** around during the week, you might have a lot of work to do on this day. __Saturday__

7. **Even** though you want to play video games, you might have to do homework during this time. __evening__

Words Across the Curriculum

Say each social studies word. Then, write the word.

1. early __early__   3. later __later__
2. history __history__   4. future __future__

Write each social studies word next to its meaning.

1. afterward __later__
2. record of events __history__
3. period of time that hasn't happened yet __future__
4. near the beginning __early__

94

Words in Writing

What plans do you have for the coming week? Write a schedule that tells what you will do next week. Use at least four words from the box.

| Friday | morning | Saturday | Monday | Thursday | later | future |
| Sunday | Tuesday | evening | afternoon | Wednesday | early | history |

Answers will vary.

Misspelled Words

Read the schedule. Circle the five misspelled words. Then, write the words correctly on the lines below.

(Sonday:) Make sure that everything is ready for the school week.
Monday: Go to baseball practice in the (afternone.)
(Tousday:) Work on my art project.
(Wensday:) Give my dog a bath.
(Thurday:) Study for the science quiz.
Friday: Clean my room after school.

__Sunday__   __Tuesday__   __Thursday__
__afternoon__   __Wednesday__

95

Say each word. Listen for vowel and consonant sounds that you know. Then, write the word. Make sure that you use a capital letter to begin each month.

| Spelling Tip | The names of months always begin with a capital letter. |

Spelling Words

March	__March__
July	__July__
May	__May__
September	__September__
January	__January__
April	__April__
June	__June__
November	__November__
August	__August__
February	__February__
October	__October__
December	__December__

96

Words in Writing

Seasons

In many parts of the country, winter begins in the month of __December__, which is the last month of the year. Often, it is cold and snowy during this month and the two following months, __January__ and __February__. Spring begins in the month of __March__. Plants begin to sprout then. They keep growing in __April__, which is often a rainy month. By __May__, many plants are flowering.

Summer begins in the month of __June__. The temperatures are warm, and they become even warmer in __July__. By __August__, the days are very hot. They begin to cool down in __September__, the first month of fall. In __October__, the days become chilly, and the leaves of the trees have changed to red, yellow, and orange. By __November__, most of the leaves have fallen from the trees. Soon, it will be winter again.

Word Building

The abbreviations for six of the months are the first three letters followed by a period. Write the abbreviations for the months below.

1. January __Jan.__   4. August __Aug.__
2. October __Oct.__   5. February __Feb.__
3. December __Dec.__   6. November __Nov.__

97

Answer Key

Page 98

Fun with Words
Write the spelling words that completes each sentence and rhymes with the words in bold.

1. **March** is the **arch** from winter to spring.
2. **April** will be filled with showers so each **day** in **May** has many flowers.
3. We enjoy the last **ember** of every fire in the chilly months of **November** and **December**.
4. **January** and **February** are very, **very** cold.
5. **June** goes by too **soon**, but **July** truly **flies** by.
6. Do you **remember** the colored leaves in **September** ?

Words Across the Curriculum
Say each science word. Then ⊙ the word.

1. season **season**   3. winter **winter**
2. calendar **calendar**   4. autumn **autumn**

Write the missing science words.

We use a **calendar** to keep track of the days, weeks, and months of the year. Every **season** of the year has three months. The last month of the year and the first two months of the next year are the **winter**. The ninth, tenth, and eleventh months are **autumn**.

98

Page 99

Words in Writing
Write a description of your favorite season. Use at least four words from the box.

| March | May | January | June | August | October | season | winter |
| July | September | April | November | February | December | calendar | autumn |

Answers will vary.

Misspelled Words
Read the description. Circle the five misspelled words. Then, write the words correctly on the lines below.

My favorite season is (autumm.) After the hot days of August, I enjoy the cooler days in (Septembar.) I love the shades of yellow, orange, and red on the trees in (Ocober.) By the end of November, I'm a little sad that (wintur) is almost here. But I also look forward to the holiday (seson) in December.

autumn   October   season
September   winter

99

Page 100

Say each holiday. Listen for vowel and consonant sounds that you know. Then, write the holiday. Make sure that you use a capital letter to begin each word of a holiday. Also make sure that you use an **'s** when it is needed.

| Spelling Tip | The names of months always begin with a capital letter. |

Spelling Words

Mother's Day   **Mother's Day**
Thanksgiving   **Thanksgiving**
Columbus Day   **Columbus Day**
Independence Day   **Independence Day**
Father's Day   **Father's Day**
Memorial Day   **Memorial Day**
Labor Day   **Labor Day**
Valentine's Day   **Valentine's Day**
Halloween   **Halloween**
New Year's Day   **New Year's Day**

100

Page 101

Words in Context
Write the missing spelling words.

Holidays

Holidays are days of celebration that come at different times during the year. **New Year's Day** is the first holiday of the year. It's celebrated on the first day of January.

Valentine's Day comes in the middle of February. This holiday stands for love.

Two holidays are celebrated in May. One is **Mother's Day**, which is a special day for mothers. The other is **Memorial Day**, the holiday that honors Americans who died in wars. The special day in June for fathers is **Father's Day**.

Independence Day is another summer holiday. We celebrate America's freedom on this day. **Labor Day** comes at the end of the summer. This day honors working people.

Columbus Day is a day in October on which we honor the explorer who discovered America. Another holiday in October is **Halloween**. On this day, people dress up in costumes and go from door to door saying "Trick or treat!" On **Thanksgiving Day**, we give thanks for everything we have.

101

Answer Key

Fun with Words

Write the holidays next to the symbols that represent them.

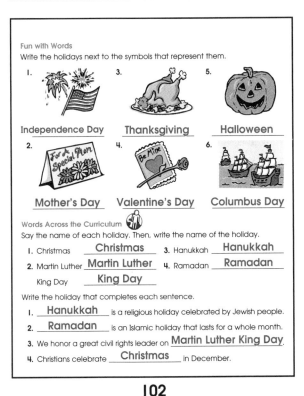

1. Independence Day
3. Thanksgiving
5. Halloween
2. Mother's Day
4. Valentine's Day
6. Columbus Day

Words Across the Curriculum

Say the name of each holiday. Then, write the name of the holiday.

1. Christmas   **Christmas**   3. Hanukkah   **Hanukkah**

2. Martin Luther **Martin Luther**   4. Ramadan   **Ramadan**
   King Day   **King Day**

Write the holiday that completes each sentence.

1. **Hanukkah** is a religious holiday celebrated by Jewish people.

2. **Ramadan** is an Islamic holiday that lasts for a whole month.

3. We honor a great civil rights leader on **Martin Luther King Day**.

4. Christians celebrate **Christmas** in December.

102

Words in Writing

Which holidays are your favorites? Write a paragraph that tells what you do on some holidays. Use at least four names of holidays from the box.

Mother's Day	Independence Day	Labor Day	New Year's Day	Martin Luther King Day
Thanksgiving	Father's Day	Valentine's Day	Christmas	Ramadan
Columbus Day	Halloween	Memorial Day	Hanukkah	

Answers will vary.

Misspelled Words

Read the paragraph. Circle the four misspelled holidays. Then, write the holidays correctly on the lines below.

One of my favorite holidays is (Haloween.) I like to carve faces in pumpkins and dress up in a scary costume. My other favorite is (Independense) Day. My family goes to a big picnic, and then we watch fireworks. I also like Thanksgiving and (Chrismas) because everyone in my family gets together on those days. (Mother Day) is another special day. I give my mom flowers and do all her chores for her.

Halloween   Christmas

Independence Day   Mother's Day

103

Write the days of the week in the correct order.

1. Sunday
2. Monday
3. Tuesday
4. Wednesday
5. Thursday
6. Friday
7. Saturday

Write the name of the holiday next to its date or description.

1. February 14   Valentine's Day
2. Fourth of July   Independence Day
3. the third Thursday in November   Thanksgiving
4. the day in June honoring dads   Father's Day
5. the day honoring Americans who have died in wars   Memorial Day
6. the first day in January   New Year's Day
7. the day that honors people who work   Labor Day
8. the day that honors moms   Mother's Day
9. the day to celebrate love   Valentine's Day
10. the day that honors the explorer who discovered America   Columbus Day

104

Write the names of the months of the year in the correct order.

1. January
2. February
3. March
4. April
5. May
6. June
7. July
8. August
9. September
10. October
11. November
12. December

Write four sentences that tell about what you like to do on your birthday. Use three spelling words that name three parts of the day.

Answers will vary.

105

Answer Key

Say each word. Listen for the **ld** or **ft** sound. Then, write the word.

Spelling Tip	The consonant blends **ft** and **ld** are spelled the way they sound.

Spelling Words

gift	gift
sold	sold
left	left
raft	raft
held	held
swift	swift
wild	wild
after	after
drift	drift
world	world

106

Words in Context
Write the missing spelling words.

Movie Review

I recently got the movie *Huckleberry Finn* as a ___**gift**___ for my birthday. The movie is about a ___**wild**___ and adventurous boy called Huck. He wants to escape from his small town and the mild-mannered but strict Widow Douglas. He longs to see more of the ___**world**___.

Huck has an older friend named Jim, who is a slave. Jim also wants to escape so that he won't be ___**sold**___ to a new owner. Huck and Jim escape from their town together when they ___**drift**___ down the ___**swift**___ water of the Mississippi River on a ___**raft**___ made of logs ___**held**___ together by ropes. ___**After**___ they ___**left**___ their small town, Huck and Jim had many adventures on the river.

Word Building
The suffix **–ness** means the **state of being**. Add the suffix **–ness** to each word to make a new word. Then, write the new word.

1. wild	**ness**	wildness
2. soft	**ness**	softness
3. swift	**ness**	swiftness
4. mild	**ness**	mildness
5. cold	**ness**	coldness

107

Fun with Words

Antonyms are words that mean the opposite of other words. Write the spelling word that is an antonym of each word below.

1. slow		swift
2. bought		sold
3. right		left
4. before		after
5. dropped		held
6. tame		wild

Words Across the Curriculum
Say each art word. Then, write the word.

1. gold	gold	3. craft	craft
2. mold	mold	4. tuft	tuft

Write the art word that correctly completes each sentence.

1. You can ___**mold**___ clay into many different shapes.

2. The color ___**gold**___ contains yellow, green, and red.

3. You can tie the ends of yarn pieces into a knot to make a ___**tuft**___.

4. Basket weaving is a ___**craft**___ that is easy to learn.

108

Words in Writing
Write a summary of a movie that you saw or a book that you read. Use at least four words from the box.

gift	left	held	wild	drift	gold	craft
sold	raft	swift	after	world	mold	tuft

Answers will vary.

Dictionary Practice
Identify each word below as being most commonly used as a **noun**, **verb**, or **adjective**. Some words can be more than one part of speech. Use the dictionary in the back if you need help.

1. gift	noun	5. swift	adjective
2. wild	adjective	6. sold	verb
3. raft	noun	7. world	noun
4. held	verb	8. drift	verb

109

Spectrum Spelling
Grade 3

Answer Key

Answer Key

Say each word. Listen to the beginning sound. Then, write the word.

Spelling Tips	The /kw/ sound is always spelled **qu**. The /skw/ sound is always spelled **squ**.

Spelling Words

quiet	quiet
quack	quack
queen	queen
squeeze	squeeze
quilt	quilt
squeak	squeak
quick	quick
squirrel	squirrel
quite	quite
question	question

110

Words in Context
Write the missing spelling words.

Stella Finally Sleeps

Challenge

Circle the other words in the story with the /kw/ or /skw/ sounds.

Once, there was a **queen** named Stella who ruled a small country. Stella was **quite** happy with her life. She had only one worry: she couldn't sleep. Every night, Stella got in her bed and covered herself with her favorite **quilt**. Stella would **squeeze** her eyes shut and try to sleep.

Even if her room was perfectly **quiet**, Stella imagined that she heard queer sounds. Sometimes, she heard the **quack** of a duck, the **squeak** of a mouse, or the squeal of a pig. Other times, she heard a **squirrel** crunching nuts with its teeth. Once, she even heard the squirt of ink from a squid swimming in the ocean.

When she heard these sounds, Stella would toss and squirm in her bed. Stella did not quit trying to answer the **question** of why she kept hearing these sounds. Finally, she solved her problem with a strange but **quick** solution. She started wearing earplugs at night.

111

Fun with Words
Write the spelling word that belongs with each pair of words.

1. silence, hush,   quiet
2. fast, swift,   quick
3. princess, king,   queen
4. blanket, cover,   quilt
5. command, exclamation, question
6. very, greatly,   quite
7. chirp, cluck,   quack
8. chipmunk, groundhog, squirrel

Words Across the Curriculum
Say each math word. Then, write the word.

1. quart   quart   3. quotient   quotient
2. quarter quarter   4. quiz   quiz

Write the math word that completes each sentence.

1. One **quarter** equals twenty-five cents.
2. It's easy to get behind in math if you don't take a **quiz** every week.
3. Two pints equal one **quart**.
4. The answer to a division problem is called a **quotient**.

112

Words in Writing
Make up a fairy tale or a short story.
Use at least four words from the box.

quiet	queen	quilt	quick	quite	quart	quotient
quack	squeeze	squeak	squirrel	question	quarter	quiz

Answers will vary.

Dictionary Practice
Write the correct symbol for the vowel sound in the first or only syllable of each word.

/a/	/ē/	/ī/
/e/	/i/	

1. squeeze   /ē/   5. quick   /i/
2. quack   /a/   6. squeak   /ē/
3. quite   /ī/   7. quiet   /ī/
4. question /e/   8. quilt   /i/

113

Page 114

Say each word. Listen to the beginning sound. Notice that the beginning letter **k** or **w** is silent. Then, write the word.

Spelling Tips	The letter **k** is silent when followed by the letter **n**. The letter **w** is silent when followed by the letter **r**.

Spelling Words

know	know
wrist	wrist
knife	knife
knob	knob
wrong	wrong
knee	knee
wrote	wrote
knock	knock
wren	wren
knight	knight

114

Page 115

Words in Context

Write the missing spelling words.

Challenge
Circle the other words in the story with silent **k** or silent **w**.

Sir Lancelot

A long time ago, a (well-known) writer

wrote an exciting story about a **knight**

named Lancelot. He was (known) as a very good man

(who) never did anything **wrong**.
Lancelot had many adventures as he rode
around the country.

One time, Lancelot came to a castle
that seemed to be empty. As Lancelot began

to **knock** on the door, the

knob turned, and a lady opened
the door. She was crying because her pet falcon

had chased a small, brown **wren** into

a tree and wouldn't come down. Lancelot put down

his (sword) and his **knife**. He took off his (armor). Then, he
made a (knot) in a rope tied to his horse's saddle and (wrapped) the rope
around the tree. Lancelot climbed the tree and held out his arm to the

falcon. It jumped onto his **wrist**. As Lancelot returned the

falcon to the lady, he bent one **knee** and (kneeled) in front

of her. He didn't **know** that an enemy was hiding in some
bushes. That began another adventure.

115

Page 116

Fun with Words

Write the spelling word that fits each clue.

1. You need me to help you open a door. — **knob**
2. I am a man, but I'm covered with metal. — **knight**
3. You have to bend me to walk. — **knee**
4. I am never right. — **wrong**
5. I can make a signal when there's no doorbell. — **knock**
6. I am a blade, but I'm not grass. — **knife**

Words Across the Curriculum

Say each language arts word. Then, write the word.

1. written — **written**
2. writing — **writing**
3. known — **known**
4. knew — **knew**

Write the language arts word that completes each sentence.

1. **Writing** is a process that includes brainstorming, drafting, writing, editing, and proofreading.
2. More than 3,000 languages are **known** to exist in the world.
3. At one time, most people who spoke English **knew** the stories of King Arthur and Sir Lancelot.
4. The legend of King Arthur and his knights was first **written** in the 1400s.

116

Page 117

Words in Writing

Imagine that you are a knight who lived long ago. Write a journal entry that tells what one of your days might be like. Use at least four words from the box.

know	knife	wrong	wrote	wren	written	known
wrist	knob	knee	knock	knight	writing	knew

Answers will vary.

Dictionary Practice

Write the word from the box that fits each pronunciation.

1. /nō/ — **know**
2. /rit´ en/ — **written**
3. /nīt/ — **knight**
4. /nē/ — **knee**
5. /nok/ — **knock**
6. /rīt´ ing/ — **writing**
7. /rōt/ — **wrote**
8. /nīf/ — **knife**

117

Answer Key

Say each word. Listen to the sounds **lf**, **mb**, and **tch**. Then, write the word.

> **Spelling Tips**
> In some words, the /f/ sound is spelled **lf**, the /m/ sound is spelled **mb**, and the /ch/ sound is spelled **tch**.

Spelling Words

half	half
thumb	thumb
match	match
climb	climb
myself	myself
scratch	scratch
pitcher	pitcher
shelf	shelf
crumb	crumb
kitchen	kitchen

118

Words in Context
Write the missing spelling words.

> **Challenge**
> Circle the other words in the narrative with **lf**, **mb**, **tch**.

Making Cookies

I like to make cookies with my parents. First, Dad (switches) on the oven. Then, I **climb** up on a stool to get the flour, sugar, and chocolate chips off the **shelf**. Next, Mom gets out the eggs and butter. I mix everything together by **myself**, and then I shape the dough into balls. When the balls are smooth, Mom slices them all in **half**. She's careful not to cut or **scratch** her fingers with the knife. I put the pieces on a cookie sheet and flatten them with my **thumb**. Then, Dad puts all the pieces in the oven and (watches) the clock for the next fifteen minutes.

Soon, the **kitchen** is filled with the wonderful smell of a (batch) of warm cookies. Dad takes them out of the oven and puts them on a plate next to a **pitcher** of milk. Everyone in my family agrees that warm cookies and cold milk are a perfect **match**. There won't be a single cookie **crumb** left in a few hours.

119

Fun with Words
Write the spelling word that answers each question.

1. Where do you put a book? **shelf**
2. What is each part of a pizza divided in two? **half**
3. In what room is the food cooked in your home? **kitchen**
4. How do you get up a tree? **climb**
5. What do you do to an itch? **scratch**
6. What is the smallest part of a cake left on a plate? **crumb**
7. What would you use to light a candle? **match**
8. What part of your hand is different from your fingers? **thumb**

Words Across the Curriculum
Say each science word. Then, write the word.

1. lamb **lamb**   3. calf **calf**
2. hatch **hatch**   4. switch **switch**

Write the science word that completes each sentence.

1. A **calf** is a baby cow.
2. Chicks **hatch** from eggs.
3. A **switch** turns the light on and off.
4. A **lamb** grows up to be a sheep.

120

Words in Writing
What kind of snacks do you like to make? Explain how you make a snack or meal. Use at least four words from the box.

half	match	myself	pitcher	crumb	lamb	calf
thumb	climb	scratch	shelf	kitchen	hatch	switch

Answers will vary.

Misspelled Words
Read the explanation. Circle the four misspelled words. Then, write the words correctly on the lines below.

When I get home from school, I go into the (kichen) to make a snack. I usually make mysel (haf) a sandwich. I cut a piece of bread in two. Then, I get some ham and cheese from a shelf in the refrigerator. I grab a (picher) of iced-tea, too. Once I put my sandwich together and pour my drink, my stomach is growling. I eat every (crum.)

kitchen	pitcher
half	crumb

121

Answer Key

Write the spelling word that means the opposite.

1. before   after
2. noisy   quiet
3. whole   half
4. answer   question
5. tame   wild
6. bought   sold

Write the spelling word that fits each pair of words.

1. bedroom, dining room,   kitchen
2. chipmunk, rabbit,   squirrel
3. fork, spoon,   knife
4. himself, yourself   myself
5. king, princess,   queen
6. leg, ankle,   knee
7. blanket, cover,   quilt
8. printed, typed   wrote

122

Write the spelling word that rhymes with each pair of words.

1. stack, back,   quack
2. missed, kissed,   wrist
3. please, breeze,   squeeze
4. so, row,   know
5. time, rhyme,   climb
6. weld, spelled,   held
7. speak, leak,   squeak
8. long, song,   wrong
9. curled, twirled,   world
10. hen, then,   wren

Answer the following questions.

1. Which two spelling words mean **fast**?
    swift   quick
2. Which two spelling words rhyme with **fight**?
    knight   quite
3. Which two spelling words rhyme with **catch**?
    match   scratch
4. Which two spelling words rhyme with **drum**?
    crumb   thumb

123

Say each word. Listen to the /âr/ sound. Then, write the word.

Spelling Tips	The /âr/ sound can be spelled air, are, and ear.

Spelling Words

care	care
wear	wear
share	share
bear	bear
hair	hair
pear	pear
chair	chair
fair	fair
dare	dare
stare	stare

124

Words in Context
Write the missing spelling words.

Fun for Everyone

Challenge

Circle the other words in the advertisement that have the /âr/ sound.

Are you (aware) that the state _____ fair _____ will be held next week? (There) will be all kinds of fun things to _____ share _____ with your family and friends. Be sure to _____ wear _____ comfortable clothes, because you will want to stay all day. (There) will be some (very) exciting rides for those who _____ dare _____ to get on them. When you need to rest from the (glare) of the sun, you can sit in a _____ chair _____ and listen to one of the bands.

You won't want to miss the (rare) black polar _____ bear _____ and he (pair) of newborn cubs. But (beware!) You must take _____ care _____ not to get too close to (their) cage. If you see the _____ hair _____ on the mother's neck rise, and she starts to _____ stare _____ at you, it's time to move on to the farm building. (There) you can see the largest apple, peach, and _____ pear _____ grown this summer.

125

Spectrum Spelling
Grade 3

Answer Key

Page 126

Fun with Words

Write the spelling word that completes each sentence and is a homophone of the word in bold.

1. Will you please **pare** a _____ pear _____ for me?
2. The cage of the _____ bear _____ is **bare**.
3. What is the **fare** to ride the bus to the _____ fair _____?
4. The **hare** has soft brown _____ hair _____ on its ears.
5. **Where** will you _____ wear _____ that hat?
6. Why did the girl _____ stare _____ at the **stair**?

Words Across the Curriculum

Say each science word. Then, write the word.

1. air _____ air _____
2. hare _____ hare _____
3. mare _____ mare _____
4. lair _____ lair _____

Write the science word that completes each sentence.

1. The _____ mare _____ is in the field with her colt.
2. A _____ hare _____ looks like a rabbit.
3. People breathe _____ air _____ into their lungs.
4. The wolf was hiding in its _____ lair _____.

Page 127

Words in Writing

What events or places do you like to go to? Write an ad about a place or event. Use at least four words from the box.

| care | share | hair | chair | dare | air | mare |
| wear | bear | pear | fair | stare | hare | lair |

Answers will vary.

Dictionary Practice

Look at each pair of guide words. Circle the word that comes between them in alphabetical order.

1. bear—bore — brake — (black) — bump
2. air—and — ask — ape — (all)
3. spare—sure — (stare) — snare — swan
4. chair—clear — cent — (city) — cost
5. slide—spoon — skip — share — (smack)
6. warm—when — (wear) — wisp — woven

Page 128

Say each word. Listen to the /ôr/ or /ûr/ sound. Then, write the word.

Spelling Tips: The /ôr/ sound can be spelled **or**, **oor**, and **ore**. The /ûr/ sound can be spelled **ir** and **ur**.

Spelling Words

dirt	dirt
order	order
door	door
worst	worst
hurt	hurt
score	score
before	before
hurry	hurry
sport	sport
nurse	nurse

Page 129

Words in Context

Write the missing spelling words.

Challenge: Circle the other words in the story with the /ôr/ or /ûr/ sound.

Ouch!

My last baseball game was the _____ worst _____ game of my life. In the ninth inning, the _____ score _____ was tied 3-3. It was my (turn) in the batting _____ order _____. I hit the ball and saw an outfielder _____ hurry _____ toward the ball. I ran to (first) base and was rounding the (corner) to second when I slipped and fell to the _____ dirt _____. I knew right away that my ankle was badly _____ hurt _____. I had never felt such pain _____ before _____ in my life.

My dad took me to the hospital and had to carry me through the _____ door _____. A _____ nurse _____ took me in a room and asked me some questions. Then, she took me to get an X-ray. Later, the doctor told me that my ankle was sprained. I had to use crutches (for) two weeks.

Still, baseball is my favorite _____ sport _____.

Word Building

The prefix **re-** means **to do again**. Add the prefix **re-** to each word to make a new word. Then, write the word.

1. **re**_order — reorder
2. **re**_fill — refill
3. **re**_pay — repay
4. **re**_read — reread
5. **re**_heat — reheat
6. **re**_start — restart
7. **re**_write — rewrite
8. **re**_view — review

Answer Key

Page 130

Fun with Words
Circle the hidden spelling words. Words can be across or down.

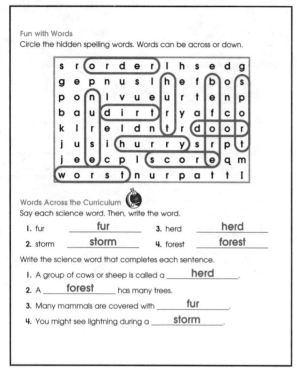

Words Across the Curriculum
Say each science word. Then, write the word.

1. fur   fur   3. herd   herd

2. storm   storm   4. forest   forest

Write the science word that completes each sentence.

1. A group of cows or sheep is called a ___herd___.

2. A ___forest___ has many trees.

3. Many mammals are covered with ___fur___.

4. You might see lightning during a ___storm___.

130

Page 131

Words in Writing
What sports do you like to play? Write a paragraph that tells about a time when you played the sport. Use at least four words from the box.

| dirt | door | hurt | before | sport | fur | herd |
| order | worst | score | hurry | nurse | storm | forest |

Answers will vary.

Misspelled Words
Read the paragraph. Circle the four misspelled words. Then, write the words correctly on the lines below.

Soccer is my favorite (sporte.) My team had a game last Monday. We practiced for a little while (befor) the game. As I was trying to (scor) a goal, I fell down and scraped my knees in the (durt.) It didn't really hurt, though. I got to play the whole game.

___sport___   ___score___

___before___   ___dirt___

131

Page 132

Say each word. Listen to the two words that make up the compound word. Then, write the word.

Spelling Tip	Compound words are made by putting two smaller words together.

Spelling Words

popcorn   popcorn

cookout   cookout

sailboat   sailboat

seashell   seashell

barefoot   barefoot

birthday   birthday

moonlight   moonlight

airplane   airplane

sandcastle   sandcastle

everything   everything

132

Page 133

Words in Context
Write the missing spelling words.

Challenge
Circle the other compound words in the journal entry.

A Great Weekend Trip

My ___birthday___ was last Saturday, so my (grandparents) took me on a (weekend) trip to the beach. We flew on an ___airplane___ to get there. When we got to our beach house, we walked ___barefoot___ on the sand. We also made a ___sandcastle___ and waded in the ocean. I found a smooth, white ___seashell___.

Later in the (afternoon,) we floated on the ocean in a ___sailboat___. Afterward, we had a ___cookout___ with (cheeseburgers) and ___popcorn___. I fed some crumbs to a (seagull.) In the evening, we walked along the (seashore) in the ___moonlight___. ___Everything___ about that day was wonderful.

Word Building
Add one of the smaller words from a spelling word to each word below to make a new compound word. Then, write the new compound word.

1. ___sea___ shore   seashore

2. ___sand___ box   sandbox

3. ___foot___ ball   football

4. sun ___light___   sunlight

5. ___cook___ book   cookbook

133

Answer Key

Fun with Words
Combine the two words in each sentence that make a compound spelling word.

1. Look at the castle made of sand.   sandcastle
2. Can you see the pale light of the moon?   moonlight
3. The corn soon began to pop loudly.   popcorn
4. When do you celebrate the day of your birth?   birthday
5. My foot was bare when I took off my sandal.   barefoot
6. Do you like to sail on a boat?   sailboat
7. Look at this shell that I found by the sea.   seashell
8. Come out so we can cook some hot dogs on the grill.   cookout

Words Across the Curriculum
Say each science word. Then, write the word.

1. eardrum   eardrum   3. snowflake   snowflake
2. rainbow   rainbow   4. backbone   backbone

Write the science word that completes each sentence.

1. A snowflake is made of tiny ice crystals.
2. Another name for an animals' spine is a backbone.
3. The eardrum allows a person to hear sounds.
4. Water drops in the sky reflect light to make a rainbow.

134

Words in Writing
What places in nature do you like? Write a description of a natural habitat you like to visit. Use at least four words from the box.

popcorn sailboat barefoot moonlight sandcastle eardrum rainbow
cookout seashell birthday airplane everything snowflake backbone

Answers will vary.

Dictionary Practice
Write the words from the box that belong in each column. Some words belong in two columns.

/ā/	/ē/	/ō/
snowflake	seashell	backbone
birthday	everything	rainbow
rainbow		sailboat
airplane		snowflake
sailboat		

135

Say each word. Listen to the two words that make up the compound word. Then, write the word.

Spelling Tip	Compound words are made by putting two smaller words together.

Spelling Words

hallway	hallway
sidewalk	sidewalk
farmhouse	farmhouse
hillside	hillside
inside	inside
springtime	springtime
driveway	driveway
cornfield	cornfield
downstairs	downstairs
horseback	horseback

136

Words in Context
Write the missing spelling words.

Challenge
Circle the other compound words in the description.

For Sale

There is an old farmhouse for sale. The house was built on a hillside. The front yard has two rows of tall trees leading from the sidewalk to the house. It also has a (flowerbed) that is filled with colorful tulips in the springtime. A long driveway leads behind the house to the garage. Behind the (backyard) is a large cornfield with stalks that grow six feet tall in the summer. There is a trail around the field where people can ride on horseback.

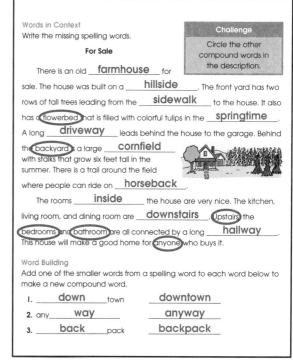

The rooms inside the house are very nice. The kitchen, living room, and dining room are downstairs. (Upstairs) the (bedrooms) and (bathroom) are all connected by a long hallway. This house will make a good home for (anyone) who buys it.

Word Building
Add one of the smaller words from a spelling word to each word below to make a new compound word.

1. down town   downtown
2. any way   anyway
3. back pack   backpack

137

Answer Key

Page 138

Fun with Words

Combine the words in the box to make eight spelling words.

| back | down | farm | hall | house | stairs | walk |
| corn | drive | field | horse | spring | time | way |

1. hallway
2. cornfield
3. downstairs
4. springtime

5. driveway
6. sidewalk
7. farmhouse
8. horseback

Words Across the Curriculum

Say each social studies word. Then, write the word.

1. railroad ___railroad___
2. stoplight ___stoplight___
3. firefighter ___firefighter___
4. crosswalk ___crosswalk___

Write each social studies word next to its definition.

1. a light that signals for car drivers to stop — stoplight
2. a track that trains run on — railroad
3. a person who puts out fires — firefighter
4. a place where people walk across a street — crosswalk

138

Page 139

Words in Writing

Write a description of where you live.
Use at least four words from the box.

| hallway | farmhouse | inside | driveway | downstairs | railroad | stoplight |
| sidewalk | hillside | springtime | cornfield | horseback | firefighter | crosswalk |

Answers will vary.

Misspelled Words

Read the description. Circle the five misspelled words. Then, write the words correctly on the lines below.

My house is in the country near a railrode track. There are only a few houses on my street, so it doesn't have a sidewak. We live next to a farmhouse that has a big cornfeld behind it. When the snow melts in the sprigtime, I get to ride in the field on horsback.

| railroad | cornfield | horseback |
| sidewalk | springtime | |

139

Page 140

Write the spelling word that is a homophone of each word below.

1. bare — bear
2. fare — fair
3. stair — stare
4. where — wear
5. pair — pear
6. hare — hair

Write the spelling word that belongs with each word.

1. doctor and nurse
2. table and chair
3. window and door
4. law and order
5. truth or dare
6. game and sport
7. before and after
8. best and worst

140

Page 141

Write the compound spelling word that fits each clue.

1. This season follows wintertime. — springtime
2. You might see this in the sky at night. — moonlight
3. You have no shoes on. — barefoot
4. You might see a scarecrow in this. — cornfield
5. Cars are sometimes parked here. — driveway
6. This is the day you were born. — birthday
7. You can ride on water in this. — sailboat
8. This is a snack that goes with movies. — popcorn
9. You walk along a street on this. — sidewalk
10. You are not outside. — inside
11. You can make this on a beach. — sandcastle
12. You can fly in the air in this. — airplane
13. This is the lower level of a house. — downstairs
14. You can sled down this in the winter. — hillside
15. You walk down this to get to your classroom. — hallway
16. You can travel this way on a ranch. — horseback

141

Notes

Notes

Notes

Notes

Notes